# YORK NOTES

# Pride and Prejudice

## Jane Austen

Note by Martin Gray & Laura Gray

Martin Gray & Laura Gray are hereby identified as authors of this work in accordance
with Section 77 of the Copyright, Designs and Patents Act 1988

YORK PRESS
322 Old Brompton Road, London SW5 9JH

PEARSON EDUCATION LIMITED
Edinburgh Gate, Harlow,
Essex CM20 2JE, United Kingdom
Associated companies, branches and representatives throughout the world

First published 2001

ISBN 0-582-32907-8

Designed by Vicki Pacey
Phototypeset by Gem Graphics, Trenance, Mawgan Porth, Cornwall
Colour reproduction and film output by Spectrum Colour
Produced by Addison Wesley Longman China Limited, Hong Kong

# CONTENTS

038083

PART FOUR

TEXTUAL ANALYSIS

PART FIVE

BACKGROUND

PART SIX

CRITICAL HISTORY & BROADER PERSPECTIVES

# PART ONE

# INTRODUCTION

## HOW TO STUDY A NOVEL

Studying a novel on your own requires self-discipline and a carefully thought-out work plan in order to be effective.

- You will need to read the novel more than once. Start by reading it quickly for pleasure, then read it slowly and thoroughly.
- On your second reading make detailed notes on the plot, characters and themes of the novel. Further readings will generate new ideas and help you to memorise the details of the story.
- Some of the characters will develop as the plot unfolds. How do your responses towards them change during the course of the novel?
- Think about how the novel is narrated. From whose point of view are events described?
- A novel may or may not present events chronologically: the time-scheme may be a key to its structure and organisation.
- What part do the settings play in the novel?
- Are words, images or incidents repeated so as to give the work a pattern? Do such patterns help you to understand the novel's themes?
- Identify what styles of language are used in the novel.
- What is the effect of the novel's ending? Is the action completed and closed, or left incomplete and open?
- Does the novel present a moral and just world?
- Cite exact sources for all quotations, whether from the text itself or from critical commentaries. Wherever possible find your own examples from the novel to back up your opinions.
- Always express your ideas in your own words.

This York Note offers an introduction to *Pride and Prejudice* and cannot substitute for close reading of the text and the study of secondary sources.

*Pride and Prejudice* is one of the most famous novels in the **canon** of English literature, constantly in print, read and reread since its publication in 1813, and made into numerous films and television adaptations. Essentially it is a love story, though we may be surprised by the frequency with which money is discussed rather than sentiment, or powerful feeling.

Elizabeth Bennet has come to be seen as one of the great heroines from the whole range of nineteenth-century novels; intelligent, sympathetic and witty, with an attitude to family life and marriage which is a model of balance, humour and good sense. With her help and some good luck, Darcy, whom she begins by hating and ends by marrying, is rescued from being a snob, hidebound by pride in his wealth and ancestry, and turned into a true gentleman.

After the novel has been enjoyed for the creation of its comic world – with Elizabeth's petty-minded, nerve-prostrated mother, her father, surrounded by women whom he regards as essentially silly, the boring, pompous Mr Collins; and the essence of all self-infatuated egocentricity, Lady Catherine de Bourgh – then the reader can start to piece together an impression of Austen's art as a narrator. The relationships between the characters, and their different reactions to the various **themes** that are introduced throughout the **plot** will be seen to be as finely patterned and balanced as are her individual sentences and paragraphs. Nothing is left to chance in its overall design. As readers we are led through the maze of manners and behaviour. We are tested and to a certain extent tricked by the appearance of things as the novel establishes its premises. This is a novel where from the first sentence **irony** is at play, and we must read carefully not to miss the sharp implications of some of Austen's comments.

We may find it difficult to sympathise with a society in which the sole function of middle-class women seems to be to marry as 'well' as possible and where the rich and powerful expect and usually receive deference from their social inferiors. We can infer also that the moral outlook of the early nineteenth-century reader is markedly different from our own. Lydia's running away with Wickham may surprise us, given her extreme youth, but we are not likely to regard her adventure as necessarily leading to her complete social downfall unless dignified by marriage, nor as a stain of wickedness which will destroy her sisters' chances of marrying well.

The focus of *Pride and Prejudice* is very narrowly domestic. The famous opening sentence makes a mock 'universal truth' out of the rapacious husband-searching in a village where there only seem to be daughters. Love and marriage are the main source of interest for the characters in the novel, and for them love and marriage have to be acceptably sanctified by society; it would be difficult to dignify even Lydia's elopement with a word like 'passion'. The inhabitants of Meryton and its environs seem untouched by history, politics or social and industrial change. Can it really have been published only sixteen years after the French Revolution, at a time when Britain was at war with France and the Napoleonic wars were raging over Europe?

# PART TWO

# Summaries & Commentaries

The text used in this Note is the Penguin Edition of *Pride and Prejudice* (1996), edited with an introduction and notes by Vivien Jones. This is based on the first edition of the novel, retaining original spellings and punctuation. As so many different texts of the novel are in use, all with different pagination, it has been judged most useful to give chapter references, rather than page references, to quotations. Some versions of the text retain the original division of the novel into three volumes, though most now have a single sequence of sixty-one chapters. The volume divisions were as below:

> Volume I   Chapters 1 to 23
> Volume II   Chapters 1 to 19 = Chapters 24 to 42
> Volume III Chapters 1 to 19 = Chapters 43 to 61

## Synopsis

Mr and Mrs Bennet, of Longbourn near Meryton, have five daughters. Jane, the eldest, is beautiful and sensible. Next in age is Elizabeth, who is clever and witty. Neither Mrs Bennet nor her daughters can inherit their house, because of a special law that dictates it must go to a male relative.

When a rich bachelor called Bingley comes to stay at nearby Netherfield Park, he is drawn into the family circle as soon as possible. Mrs Bennet devises stratagems to bring the young people together. Jane falls in love with Bingley, and Bingley seems to return Jane's love. Elizabeth takes a strong dislike to Darcy, Bingley's friend, who is wealthy but proud.

The militia comes to Meryton and the two youngest Bennet girls, Kitty and Lydia, flirt with the officers. Elizabeth is charmed by a newcomer called Wickham. Wickham grew up with Darcy, but detests him. Darcy cruelly deprived him of a career in the church.

Bingley suddenly departs for London, leaving Jane miserable. Meanwhile Mr Collins, who will inherit their house, comes to visit the Bennets. He is a disagreeably pompous clergyman and has decided to marry one of the Bennet sisters. He proposes to Elizabeth, who refuses him. He successfully turns his attentions to Charlotte Lucas, Elizabeth's friend.

Jane goes to stay in London with her aunt and uncle Gardiner, hoping to see Bingley. Elizabeth goes to stay with Charlotte Collins in Kent. Caroline Bingley, who had been so friendly to Jane in Meryton, is now cold and distant.

In Kent Elizabeth meets Darcy again, who is staying with his aunt, Lady Catherine de Bourgh. Darcy proposes marriage to her. Tactlessly he emphasises the vulgarity of Elizabeth's family in the midst of his proud declaration of love. She angrily refuses him.

In a haughty letter, Darcy justifies making Bingley stop seeing Jane: he thought she was not in love. He also spells out the true history of Wickham, who is in fact a spendthrift and a seducer. Darcy's young sister Georgiana has been a victim of Wickham's false charm.

Back at Longbourn Elizabeth disapproves of Lydia's going to stay in Brighton, where the militia's new camp is.

Elizabeth goes on a holiday tour with the Gardiners. They visit Pemberley, Darcy's impressive country estate. To her embarrassment Darcy unexpectedly turns up. He is astonishingly kind to her. Then bad news arrives: Lydia has run away with Wickham.

Elizabeth rushes back to Longbourn. Mr Gardiner goes to help her father try to find the fugitives in London. A deal is made with Wickham to make him marry Lydia. Lydia and Wickham visit the family and are unashamed of their behaviour.

Elizabeth learns from Mrs Gardiner that it was Darcy who helped to find Wickham and provided the money to make him marry Lydia. Bingley moves back to Netherfield, courts Jane, and proposes. Darcy has accompanied him, and also visits the Bennets, but seems less keen on Elizabeth than he was at Pemberley. Lady Catherine makes a surprise visit. She is intent on preventing Elizabeth marriage's to her nephew Darcy, of which she has heard rumours.

Elizabeth grasps an opportunity to thank Darcy for his secret activities on behalf of Lydia. He proposes to her again and is accepted.

**Mr Bennet**, estate yielding £2,000 per annum, entailed to **Mr Collins** due to lack of male heir
**Mrs Bennet**, father an attorney, inherited £4,000, providing income of about £160 per annum
**Jane** (Miss Bennet), 22 years old
**Elizabeth** (Lizzie, Eliza), 20 years old
**Mary**
**Catherine** (Kitty)
**Lydia**, 15/16 years old
All will inherit about £1000 'in the 4 per cents' on the death of their mother; i.e. a potential income of £40 per annum

**Mrs Philips**, Mrs Bennet's sister
**Mr Gardiner** (Edward), in trade, Mrs Bennet's brother
**Mrs Gardiner** (M.), (four young children)
**Mr Collins**, nephew of Mr Bennet, due to inherit Longbourn, marries Charlotte Lucas

**Sir William Lucas**, ex-mayor of Meryton
**Charlotte Lucas**, his daughter, Elizabeth Bennet's friend

**Mr Bingley** (Charles), inherited £100,000, looking for an estate, income therefore about £4,000 per annum
**Miss Bingley** (Caroline), his sister, inherited £20,000, income therefore about £800 per annum
**Mrs Hurst** (Louisa), his other sister, also inherited £20,000

**Colonel Forster**, marriage reported in Chapter 12, his regiment stationed at Meryton, then Brighton
**Mrs Forster** (Harriet), Lydia Bennet's friend

**Mr Darcy** (Fitzwilliam), friend of Mr Bingley, owner of Pemberley, providing income of £10,000 per annum
**Miss Darcy** (Georgiana), his sister, 16 years old

**Mr Wickham** (George), connected with Darcy family, marries Lydia for her inheritance of £1,000, plus another £1,000, plus payment of over £1,000 debts, plus purchase of a commission

**Lady Catherine de Bourgh**, widow, aunt of Darcy and Colonel Fitzwilliam, lives at Rosings, neighbour and patroness of Mr Collins
**Miss De Bourgh** (Anne), her daughter, 'betrothed' to Mr Darcy

# DETAILED SUMMARIES

CHAPTER 1    **Mr Bennet is encouraged by his wife to visit
Mr Bingley, the new bachelor in the area. An insight
into the Bennet's marriage**

Mrs Bennet is eager that her husband should pay a visit to Netherfield
Park. The new tenant of this property, Mr Bingley, is both single and
rich. Mrs Bennet hopes that he can be prevailed upon to marry one of her
five daughters. She begs her husband to pave the way for an exchange of
courtesies, but Mr Bennet teases her and appears to refuse her request.

The first and last paragraphs of the chapter have a special **register**
and perspective, sandwiching the representation of Mr and Mrs
Bennet's **dialogue** that takes up most of the chapter. The book
begins with what seems to be an **aphorism**: it is a universal truth
that 'a single man in possession of a good fortune must be in want
of a wife'. This detached opening offers an **ironic** statement about
the **themes** of the novel. Austen subverts the apparent seriousness
of a 'truth universally acknowledged' with the smallness and relative
frivolity of her subject matter. The topics of money and marriage
('fortune' and 'wife'), are introduced in relation to 'truth' and who
should acknowledge it. But the universe is immediately reduced to
a provincial neighbourhood and its families, and the need to marry
off daughters as well as possible. We must be on our guard not to
be taken in by the narrator's playfully ironic approach.

The chapter ends as it began: with a paragraph of **authorial
intervention**. Jane Austen describes Mr and Mrs Bennet and
the relative incompatibility of their characters in a series of
balanced and pithy sentences. The reader is perhaps a little
surprised by the severity with which Mrs Bennet is summed up
('mean understanding, little information and uncertain temper').
See Narrative Techniques: Style and Language for further
discussion of this passage.

This first chapter introduces the moral framework of the novel as a
whole. What are the values by which Mr and Mrs Bennet consider
their daughters? Jane is handsome; Lydia is good-humoured.
Mr Bennet dismisses them all as 'silly and ignorant, like other girls',
but commends Lizzy for her 'quickness'. What are the values that

we as readers are asked to bring to bear on the Bennets? Mr Bennet stands back from his wife, and quietly enjoys his superiority through his teasing mockery. We as readers have to do the same. The text forces us to adopt Mr Bennet's and the narrator's **ironic** stance, but in case we have missed the point, we are finally told what to think of them. The understanding of character – in which Mrs Bennet so complacently fails – is in the **foreground** as a proper occupation for an intelligent mind. As for 'truth' (and for that matter goodness, which is a value so far left out of the picture) and pride, and prejudice, the reader must await the development of events.

CHAPTER 2    **Bingley has been visited. A family discussion ensues**

Mr Bennet has already visited Bingley; teasingly he does not tell his wife immediately. We meet some of the daughters. Elizabeth's assessment of the intended visit shows her to be more measured and reasonable than her mother. Mrs Bennet takes out her vexation by scolding Kitty for coughing. Mary's seriousness is the butt of her father's ironic humour. She 'read[s] great books, and makes extract[s]' but is not clever. Finally when Mrs Bennet is told of the visit, she is in 'raptures', praises her husband and imagines her youngest daughter, Lydia, dancing with Bingley.

Except for fragmentary authorial summaries at the start and finish, again the main substance of this short chapter is **dialogue**. It could be written as a play: like a theatre audience, we have to be sensitive to nuance and irony, and imagine the characters only from their contribution to the discussion.

The comedy here grows out of Mr Bennet's continued concealment of his actions, and his deliberate misinterpretation of his wife's comments. This is a scene in which characterisation is developed by showing several different reactions to a situation: firstly the apparent refusal of Mr Bennet to visit Bingley, and secondly the joyful excitement that the visit has taken place. Similar examples of this economic (and common) method of differentiating character can be found in Chapter 5, in which pride is the subject of discussion, and Chapter 13 where a variety of responses to Mr Collins's letter are depicted.

CHAPTER 3    **Bingley repays Mr Bennet's visit. The ball takes place.
Bingley dances twice with Jane Bennet. His friend
Darcy is discovered to be proud**

Mr Bennet refuses to give a satisfactory description of Bingley.
However Sir William and Lady Lucas describe him as 'quite young,
wonderfully handsome, extremely agreeable' and everyone is
particularly pleased that he should plan to attend the next social
gathering.

The visit has been returned, but Bingley does not meet the Bennet
daughters, who spy on him from an upstairs window. He is invited to
dinner but cannot accept because he must go to London. Rumour has it
that he will attend the ball with a large party. Only five enter the
ballroom: Bingley, his two sisters, one with a husband, and one other
man. This last is a Mr Darcy: news that he is the possessor of ten
thousand pounds a year spreads rapidly around the ballroom. For a
moment he promises to be more popular than Bingley, but he is soon
dismissed for being too proud. Bingley pleases the company by dancing
all the dances, while Darcy only dances with Bingley's sisters. He ignores
everyone else.

A particular incident leads to him being reviled by the Bennet
family, since he has snubbed Elizabeth. Bingley urged Darcy to dance,
but he declares that this would be a 'punishment'. He describes Elizabeth
as merely 'tolerable' and refuses to be introduced. Later Elizabeth makes
a joke of this story with her friends, exemplifying her good humour and
delight in anything 'ridiculous'.

Mr Bennet, still awake when the family return to their home, listens
impatiently to his wife's enthusiastic report of the ball, and the fineries of
the Bingley sisters' clothes. She relates Darcy's rudeness to Elizabeth and
declares that she detests him.

> Bingley and Darcy are established as contrasting characters. Darcy's
> pride has obvious thematic implications with the novel's title. We
> see the quick fluctuations of public opinion. Mrs Bennet seems to
> judge people only by their clothes and appearance, till Darcy's sour
> manners controvert his exterior polish. The desire to dance is used
> as an index to a character's amiability.

We see Bingley and Jane Bennet paired, and suspect that Elizabeth and Darcy are due in some way for each other. But as novel readers, we guess that things are not going to go smoothly.

CHAPTER 4   **Bingley's financial situation. He and Darcy are compared, and so are Jane and Elizabeth**

Jane and Elizabeth discuss Bingley, and then his sisters. Elizabeth thinks them rude and stand-offish while Jane is determined to think well of everyone. Bingley's sisters are rich and proud. Bingley has inherited almost a hundred thousand pounds, wealth that has been acquired by trade. Bingley's father meant to purchase an estate but died, leaving this task to his son. For the moment Bingley is only the tenant of Netherfield. The characters of Bingley and Darcy are opposed. Bingley is easy-going and amiable and trusts his friend's judgement entirely, while Darcy is cleverer but 'haughty' and 'reserved'. Bingley's character brings him popularity while Darcy is likely to give offence. Their reaction to the ball illustrates these differences: Bingley is pleased by his new Meryton friends, while Darcy is scornful and critical of everything. The Bingley sisters give Jane their qualified approval as a 'sweet' girl.

This chapter focuses on Bingley, Darcy, Jane and Elizabeth, the four main characters of the novel. The generous dispositions of Jane and Bingley are explored, in contrast to the lively cynicism of Elizabeth and the haughtiness of Darcy. We are shown Jane's candour and seriousness and Elizabeth's playful humour combined with respect and love for her sister, and we are told about the two men.

Elizabeth shares her father's taste for **irony**: young men, she remarks, must be handsome 'if they possibly can'.

Her silent thoughts merge imperceptibly with authorial commentary and summary. Austen is using her as a **centre of consciousness**: we tend to see developments from her point of view.

The chapter about character is full of abstract words denoting moral qualities and behaviour: manners, ease, gallantry, candour, openness, ductility, understanding. (For further discussion of this aspect of Austen's writing see Narrative Techniques: Style and Language.)

**candour** in Austen's time, this means 'purity; integrity; freedom from bias or malice', rather that its present day meaning of 'frankness; outspokenness'

**Miss Bennet** the oldest daughter has the right to be called Miss Bennet; the others are Miss *Elizabeth* Bennet, Miss *Mary* Bennet etc

CHAPTER 5    **The Lucas family visit the Bennets and discuss the ball. Darcy is out of favour**

We learn about the Lucas family and their background. The father, Sir William, received his knighthood and retired from trade. They live very near the Bennets and the eldest daughter, Charlotte, is a particular friend of Elizabeth's. The Miss Lucases pay a visit in order to discuss the ball. Their conversation is polite but competitive. Mrs Bennet is determined to believe that Bingley has particularly favoured Jane, and negotiates the conversation in this direction. Darcy is criticised, and Jane, believing good of everyone, tries to moderate the complaints. Darcy's snubbing of Elizabeth is discussed: she vows never to dance with him. Miss Lucas suggests that he is proud but that this vice is mitigated by his having a right to be so. Mary Bennet sermonises in a boring way on the nature of pride and vanity.

Pride, one of the explicit **themes** of the novel, is discussed variously here. The introductory summary of Sir William Lucas is a masterpiece of ironic portraiture. The narrator implies that he is blown up by his knighthood, for which he did practically nothing; he is snobbish, conceited and empty-headed. Yet surprisingly though 'elated by his rank' he was 'all attention to everybody': he is friendly, obliging and courteous. By this complexity Austen adds some depth to what seemed to start as a **satiric caricature**.

Mrs Bennet's artless conversational powers are often characterised by an incapacity to complete her train of thought. Here she betrays how much she is jumping to conclusions about the future of Bingley's admiration for Jane, while simultaneously denying that she is doing so: 'that does seem as if—but however, it may all come to nothing, you know'. Mrs Bennet's slapdash incoherence is in sharp contrast with the verbal powers of the narrator, and of intelligent characters such as Elizabeth.

CHAPTER 6   **Bingley and Jane are falling in love. Elizabeth and Charlotte Lucas discuss courtship and marriage. Darcy becomes interested in Elizabeth. Miss Bingley is interested in Darcy**

The Bennet women visit Netherfield, and Bingley's sisters repay the visit. Elizabeth still does not like them, but they are kind to Jane, proof, Elizabeth thinks, of Bingley's interest in Jane. Jane is falling in love but such is her 'composure of temper and ... uniform cheerfulness of manner' that only those who know her well would know. In discussion with Elizabeth, Charlotte Lucas suggests that Jane is too guarded and self-controlled and that she risks losing Bingley by not encouraging him more openly. Elizabeth defends Jane's modesty. Charlotte's view of marriage is negative and mercenary.

Darcy has started to change his mind about Elizabeth. He is struck by her intelligence and the beauty of her dark eyes. At a party at the Lucas household he listens to her conversation with others. Elizabeth and Mary play the piano and sing. Sir William discusses dancing with Darcy and tries to persuade him to dance with Elizabeth, who, embarrassed, refuses.

Miss Bingley sidles over to Darcy and expresses her disgust at the evening. Darcy tells her that he was meditating on a pair of 'fine eyes'. On hearing that the eyes in question are those of Elizabeth Bennet, she needles him about an imagined marriage and his prospective mother-in-law. He takes no notice.

Austen clearly wishes to debate what is the appropriate behaviour of young women who are on the brink of courtship. How soon they should allow themselves to give way to and give away their feelings. How much should they leave their suitors to make the running; how much should they lead them on? The unfolding of the **plot** will show whether either Charlotte or Elizabeth is correct.

Charlotte Lucas's pessimistic, non-romantic and even cynical attitude to the chance of happiness in marriage requires attention – a 'share of vexation' seems unavoidable in wedlock, however well the parties might know each other. Elizabeth laughs off this view as 'not sound'.

The narrator enters Darcy's consciousness to show the way he is drawn to admire Elizabeth in spite of all his adverse judgements about her beauty and personality. Indeed at the very moment he endorses his criticisms to himself, he is disarmed by the contrariety of his feelings. His pride and prejudice are being subtly undone by 'a pair of fine eyes in the face of a pretty woman'. But Elizabeth, spurned at the first dance, is now filled with wounded pride and prejudice against him. Such misalignment of views has much comic potential.

There is an interesting mixture of **omniscient narratorial** understanding (Darcy's changed feelings) with dramatised **dialogue** left for the reader to interpret, though hints abound. The narrator draws attention to Darcy's 'great intrepidity' in revealing Elizabeth as the subject of his meditations. His disclosure results in Miss Bingley's poisonous and impertinent teasing. Is this a comment on Elizabeth and Charlotte's conversation about the pros and cons of revealing or concealing feelings of interest towards men?

CHAPTER 7   **The Bennets' financial and social standing is described. Jane is invited to Netherfield. She catches a cold and has to stay there, as Mrs Bennet planned. Elizabeth walks there**

Mr Bennet's property brings him two thousand pounds a year, but on his death both his estate and this income will be inherited by a distant male relative. Mrs Bennet's father was an attorney and she was left four thousand pounds. Her sister, Mrs Philips, is married to her father's clerk and successor; and her brother lives in London.

We learn that Catherine and Lydia often walk to the nearby town of Meryton. They are both excited that a regiment of militia has taken up headquarters in the town. Their aunt, Mrs Philips, introduces them to the officers, and they are obsessed by this new society. Mr Bennet accuses them of being silly, while Mrs Bennet defends them, citing her former fondness for a 'red coat'.

Jane is invited to Netherfield. Mrs Bennet insists that Jane go by horseback, in the hopes that she will be unable to return home because of the impending rain. The plan works, though Jane is made ill by the soaking she receives. Elizabeth decides to walk over to see her sister on receipt of the news. Elizabeth's appearance in the breakfast parlour at Netherfield creates much surprise. She has walked three miles on her own in unpleasant weather. Darcy silently admires the 'brilliancy' of her complexion. Jane is ill, but overjoyed to see Elizabeth. In the afternoon Elizabeth prepares to leave, but is invited to stay at Netherfield. She accepts and sends for clothes.

A good example of Austen's **irony**, where she says quite the opposite of what she means, is to be found in her icy condemnation of Mrs Bennet's plan, and its unfortunate outcome for Jane, as 'all the felicity of her contrivance'.

Austen is precise and detailed in exposing the incomes of her various characters, and the means by which their wealth has been procured. Each male character (and here Mrs Bennet too) is placed exactly according to a scale of money and respectability. As anticipated in the first sentence of the novel, the **themes** of fortune and marriage are linked; we see Mrs Bennet pricing Lydia, and risking Jane's health in order to thrust her into Bingley's company.

CHAPTER 8   **Jane is no better. Miss Bingley mocks Elizabeth's behaviour and family. Darcy's estate, library and sister are described. The ideal qualities of an accomplished woman are discussed**

Bingley's anxiety on Jane's behalf is obvious. When Elizabeth leaves the room, Miss Bingley criticises her appearance and her manners. Mrs Hurst comments adversely on how 'wild' Elizabeth looked after the walk; they discuss her dirty petticoat. Miss Bingley tries to involve Darcy in the dispraise of Elizabeth but with little success. The vulgarity of the Bennets' relations are a source of laughter between the two sisters, despite their declared regard for Jane.

In the evening Elizabeth chooses not to join the rest of the party at cards. Her preference for reading a book causes surprise. The smallness of the Bingley library is commented upon, in comparison to the wealth of books owned by Darcy. His estate, Pemberley in Derbyshire, is admired by everyone, especially Miss Bingley. Elizabeth puts down her book to listen. Miss Bingley inquires flatteringly after Darcy's young sister, Georgiana. They discuss the requisites for an 'accomplished' woman. Elizabeth doubts the possibility of any women arriving at the long list of talents and attributes that are recommended. Darcy remarks that he dislikes female cunning employed for 'captivation': Miss Bingley is discomforted. Jane's cold is even worse.

> Austen uses the discussion about libraries to establish the difference between Darcy and Bingley. The latter is portrayed as something of an upstart with his meagre library, a result of his family's recently acquired wealth. Darcy's library has been the work of generations. Reading and books, like dancing and money, are motifs which reappear in the novel (Chapters 11 and 12). Interestingly Mr Bennet is an avid reader, with an extensive library (Chapter 3 and 19).

CHAPTER 9    **Mrs Bennet visits Netherfield and embarrasses Elizabeth**

Jane is slightly better, and Elizabeth sends word to Longbourn for her mother to visit. Having assured herself that Jane is not very ill, Mrs Bennet will not allow her to return home. Mrs Bennet contradicts Darcy over the relative merits of town and country life, revealing her provincial attitude. Elizabeth is embarrassed at her mother's folly. Bingley is polite throughout the visit but his sisters are cold and ungracious. Mrs Bennet boasts about Jane's beauty and good nature, and tells of a former suitor. Elizabeth tries to change the subject by a witty comment on love and poetry. Finally Lydia Bennet asks Bingley if he will keep his promise and organise a ball. He agrees and sets the date for after Jane's recovery.

> Austen handles the complications of this scene with consummate skill. Every comment and nuance adds to our understanding of the characters' feelings and attitudes: Mrs Bennet's ignorant prattle, Bingley's friendly warmth, his sisters' disdain, Darcy's reserve,

caught as he is between growing admiration for Elizabeth and contempt for her mother, and Elizabeth's consciousness that her mother is making a fool of herself, tempered and confused by family loyalty. Such a variety of divided purposes is typical of social comedy, yet there is an underlying aspect of pain in the apparently insurmountable gulfs that separate the characters.

CHAPTER 10    **An evening in the Bingley drawing room. Bingley and Darcy are contrasted again. Miss Bingley is at her worst**

Jane's health is slowly improving. During the evening Miss Bingley attempts to obtain Darcy's attention but fails. The writing styles of Bingley and Darcy are compared. Darcy's letters are studied efforts, full of 'words of four syllables' whereas Bingley's are careless and abbreviated. Bingley's yielding nature comes in for serious discussion between Darcy and Elizabeth; the latter holds her own in the argument, which Bingley brings abruptly to an end. For a moment Darcy is nearly offended and Elizabeth checks her laughter. Elizabeth notices that Darcy is continually observing her and wonders what she is doing wrong to attract his notice. She does not imagine that he could be admiring her. He asks her if she would like to dance and, thinking he is trying to trap her into an expression of levity, she replies very pertly.

The next day Miss Bingley, in her jealousy, tries to 'provoke' Darcy by talking about his supposed marriage with Elizabeth. She comments on the flirtatious behaviour of the younger Bennet girls and on the inferiority of Elizabeth's relations.

In this chapter Darcy comes to the realisation that paying too much attention to Elizabeth could be a 'danger' were it not for 'the inferiority of her connections'. In Chapter 8 he acknowledged the detrimental effect on marriage for those with vulgar relations. Austen shows the reader that Darcy is very much aware how careful he must be in the choice of a wife. The build-up of this aspect of his character, his pride, makes the eventual resolution of the novel more surprising. But here it is Darcy who is surprised to find himself 'so bewitched'.

The polarity of Darcy and Bingley is re-emphasised. The degree to which Bingley's easy-going nature allows him to be influenced is of course directly relevant to future events.

CHAPTER 11   **Jane is better. Darcy's interest in Elizabeth increases. Elizabeth and Darcy discuss whether he is faultless. Miss Bingley is still jealous**

Jane is well enough to join the others in the drawing room. Elizabeth notes how Bingley takes care of Jane and is pleased. This evening they do not play cards. Darcy is reading, but Miss Bingley is intent on obtaining his attention. She interrupts him, he answers and then resumes his reading. Only when Elizabeth joins her for a walk around the room does Darcy put his book down. Elizabeth and Darcy discuss whether Darcy can or cannot be laughed at. She **ironically** concludes that Darcy is too perfect to be laughed at. He thinks that he is rightly proud, concedes that his temperament is 'too little yielding' and that he bears grudges. Elizabeth accuses him of hating everybody, and he accuses her of wilfully misunderstanding them. Darcy begins to appreciate the 'danger of paying Elizabeth too much attention'.

Drawing room conversation takes up almost all of this chapter. Caroline Bingley's attempts to attract Darcy's attention to herself are becoming more desperate. The reader notes that when Elizabeth joins in the conversation he is instantly interested. Can Elizabeth not have observed this too?

For a discussion of the final paragraphs, in which Darcy comments on 'pride', see Textual Analysis: Text 1

CHAPTER 12   **Jane and Elizabeth return to Longbourn. Only Bingley is sorry to see them go**

Mrs Bennet refuses Elizabeth's request for a carriage to be sent: she wants Jane to spend as long as possible in the company of Bingley. The sisters ask to borrow the Bingley carriage. They are prevailed upon to stay another night by Bingley. Darcy is pleased that Elizabeth is going and pointedly ignores her in case she guesses the effect that she has had on him.

CHAPTER 12 continued

They arrive home. Mrs Bennet is cross that they have not stayed longer, but their father is pleased to have them back at home. Mary is studying and is as pedantic as ever. We learn of Catherine and Lydia's latest discoveries regarding the officers and their movements.

Little of this chapter is dramatised – unusually there is no **dialogue** It provides an interesting example of Austen's **omniscient narration**. Darcy's peculiar behaviour in relation to Elizabeth, refusing even to look at her, is not commented upon (though the reader must wonder what to feel about it). However, the narrator's description of Mary, and her 'thread-bare morality', is clearly judgemental.

The chapter concludes with a chilling list of the young Bennets' excitements: dinners, a flogging and an impending marriage.

CHAPTER 13   **Mr Collins's letter announces his proposed visit. His arrival and manners are described**

Mr Bennet tells his family that his cousin, Mr Collins, is coming to dinner. It is he who will inherit the Longbourn property on the death of Mr Bennet. Mr Bennet has never met Collins because of a quarrel with his father. Mrs Bennet cannot bear the thought of him or the entailment of the property. In his letter Mr Collins explains that he is a clergyman in the patronage of a Lady Catherine de Bourgh in Hunsford in Kent. He hints at a way of resolving the problem of the entailment and proposes to visit the family for a week.

Mr Collins is punctual and formal. He compliments Mrs Bennet on the beauty of her daughters in very conventional terms. Once again, he hints self-importantly at the possibility of making amends to the family. He is all admiration for Longbourn and its contents.

After the reading of Mr Collins's letter, the Bennets all react to its style and content. These comments and reactions are used to contrast their characters and perceptions. Mrs Bennet is immediately placated (not least because his heavy hints suggest he is thinking of marrying one of her girls), Jane approves of his good intentions, Elizabeth questions his sense, Mary commends his clichéed composition and Catherine and Lydia are not interested as he is not a soldier. Mr Bennet meanwhile looks forward to the quiet enjoyment of Mr Collins's folly. So does the reader.

The chapter is structured in such a way as to manoeuvre the reader into a clear understanding of what kind of person Mr Collins is. His letter reveals an astonishing pomposity. The sentences are long-winded and leaden, with too many clauses. Its sentiments and style reveal a degree of self-importance and snobbery that borders on **parody**. Later, the way in which Mr Collins's conversation is related, rather than reproduced, denies vitality to his character.

CHAPTER 14 **Mr Collins describes Lady Catherine de Bourgh**

Led on by Mr Bennet, Mr Collins praises his patroness, Lady Catherine de Bourgh, and her kindness to him, which he regards as unusual, given her rank. She has advised him to get married, and her interest in his welfare extends even to the improvement of his kitchen cupboards. Mr Bennet quietly makes fun of him. His **ironic** teasing is only shared by Elizabeth (and the reader).

Mr Collins is invited to read to the company. He chooses a book of sermons. Lydia is soon bored and rudely interrupts him. Collins is much offended and refuses to continue, preferring backgammon with Mr Bennet.

Mr Collins's objection to reading a novel is not an untypical reaction for a serious clergyman in the early nineteenth century, though it may be contrasted with some of his other behaviour; is backgammon more worthwhile than reading fiction or dancing? (see Chapter 17). Of course, for such a character to make this point from within the pages of a novel is itself comic. Who reads, and what they read is a matter for debate at several points in the novel (compare, for example, the discussion in Chapter 8).

CHAPTER 15    Mr Collins's character; his plan to marry a Bennet
daughter. A walk to Meryton. Elizabeth meets Mr
Wickham. Darcy and Wickham recognise one
another. A party is planned

Mr Collins's stupidity is described and accounted for in terms of his poor education. He plans to marry one of the Bennet daughters, thereby resolving the problem of the entailment. When Mrs Bennet warns him off Jane, he decides to focus on Elizabeth. Mrs Bennet is excited at soon having two daughters married.

Elizabeth meets Mr Wickham, who is very agreeable and handsome. Darcy and Bingley pass by on horseback and Bingley inquires after Jane's health. Darcy and Mr Wickham seem to recognise one another, but both look discomforted by the meeting. Elizabeth notices and is eager to know the history of their acquaintance.

Mr Collins is presented to Mrs Philips. He is overly polite and verbose. A dinner is planned to which Wickham will be invited.

Mr Collins's mixture of 'pride and obsequiousness, self-importance and humility' is condemned outright by the narrator in the sketch of his circumstances with which the chapter starts. His easy and swift transference of this interest from one daughter to another is almost shocking in its complacence, and requires no authorial comment. The detail that he manages this change in the time that Mrs Bennet took to poke the fire is condemnation enough.

With the entry of Wickham into the narrative, and Darcy's strange reaction to their meeting, a mystery is introduced that will take a large part of the book to solve. Suspense is generated for Elizabeth and the reader: 'What could be the meaning of it?—It was impossible to imagine; it was impossible not to long to know'.

CHAPTER 16    Elizabeth is very favourably impressed by Wickham.
He tells of mistreatment by Darcy

The Longbourn party go by coach to Mrs Philips's house. Collins, intending a compliment, compares the drawing room to the small breakfast parlour at Rosings, Lady Catherine de Bourgh's estate. Mrs Philips soon realises that he is a tedious snob.

Mr Wickham's arrival at the party pleases everybody. He sits next to Elizabeth, and proves a very affable and talkative companion. Elizabeth tells him that she thinks Darcy is 'very disagreeable', and he explains his acquaintance with him. Wickham's father was steward of the Darcy estate. Wickham was a favourite of Darcy's late father, who promised him a good living in the church. The current Darcy has deprived him of his promising career as a clergyman. Wickham paints a black picture of Darcy's behaviour and nature. Elizabeth is outraged, and they discuss Darcy's excessive pride. We discover that Lady Catherine de Bourgh is Darcy's aunt and that he is destined to marry her daughter. Wickham criticises Lady Catherine, confirming Elizabeth's impression of her conceit. Elizabeth leaves the party thinking only of Wickham, and the injustice that has been perpetrated against him.

This is the longest chapter so far, and consists almost entirely of the conversation between Elizabeth and Wickham which focuses on Darcy's pride, in the context of the evening's entertainment at her aunt's. Given what happens in the novel, this encounter must be examined in detail: should Elizabeth have recognised something in Wickham's manner that might have betrayed his true nature? Does her prejudice against Darcy blind her to the inappropriate frankness of Wickham's conversation? How much is she swayed by Wickham's pleasing appearance?

**fish** counters used in board and card games

CHAPTER 17  **Jane and Elizabeth discuss Darcy. The Netherfield ball is anticipated with excitement**

Elizabeth tells Jane about Wickham's story. Jane is reluctant to believe ill of Darcy and attributes his behaviour to some misunderstanding. Bingley arrives to invite the Bennet girls to a ball at Netherfield. His sisters ignore Mrs Bennet and Elizabeth as much as they can.

Elizabeth looks forward to dancing with Wickham. However, Mr Collins asks Elizabeth to dance the first two dances with him. Elizabeth has to accept but is not pleased with the arrangement. She realises that she is the object of his marital intentions, with her mother's approval.

Elizabeth and Jane differ in their view of Wickham's assertions. Jane always tries to see the best in everyone; Elizabeth has a less charitable view of human behaviour, and is perfectly certain in her condemnation of Darcy: 'one knows exactly what to think'. Even at a first reading, it is possible to guess that events may prove her prejudice wrong. But so far our sympathies are all with Elizabeth who seems to have the same kind of intelligent (if **ironic**) grasp of events as her father and the narrator. Perhaps a clue to future events is provided by the sisters' assumption that 'veracity' and an 'amiable appearance' necessarily go together in young men. At a second reading, it is clear that the narrator views Elizabeth ironically in these scenes with Wickham. But we are being a little tricked; just like Elizabeth, we are being led astray. Every effort is made to darken Darcy and make Wickham delightful and oppressed.

CHAPTER 18    Mr Wickham is not at the ball. Elizabeth dances with Darcy. Elizabeth's family behaves badly. Jane is sure of Bingley's regard

Mr Wickham is not present at the ball. Elizabeth is disappointed and angry with Darcy. She can hardly be civil to him. Dancing with Collins proves to be a mortifying experience. Elizabeth is talking to Charlotte Lucas when they are surprised by Darcy and, almost by mistake, Elizabeth accepts his offer for a dance. Conversation is sticky, but Elizabeth refers to Wickham. Darcy is troubled by her interest and changes the subject after remarking that Wickham makes friends easily, but loses them too. Sir William Lucas speaks of the certainty of a wedding between Jane and Bingley. Darcy scrutinises them. Miss Bingley tells Elizabeth that Wickham has treated Darcy in a most 'infamous manner' and makes pointed remarks about Elizabeth's supposed interest in him. Jane reports more criticism of Wickham, this time from Bingley, but Elizabeth distrusts this opinion as coming from Darcy. Jane believes that Bingley admires her and is very happy. Collins realises that Darcy is a relation of Lady Catherine and pays him his respects against Elizabeth's advice. Darcy receives him with cold astonishment, but Collins is satisfied.

At supper Elizabeth is placed near her mother. She is embarrassed to see Mrs Bennet whispering to Lady Lucas about her hopes for Jane's marriage to Bingley. Darcy is also overhearing every word but Elizabeth cannot silence her mother. After supper Mary sings for too long, and only stops after a remonstration from her father. Collins makes a superfluous speech on music and the duties of the clergy. He pays Elizabeth much attention. Charlotte Lucas often joins them and talks to Collins herself, for which diversion Elizabeth is grateful.

The Bennets are the last to leave and Elizabeth notes how unwelcome their presence is to their hosts, with the exception of Bingley. Mrs Bennet invites Bingley to dinner and is already planning her two oldest daughters' weddings.

This is another long chapter, containing a great deal of action and information, all presented through Elizabeth's experience of the ball. Her **dialogue** with Darcy is presented in detail.

Elizabeth considers that Darcy is exhibiting prejudice towards Wickham. In retrospect we can see that it is her who is prejudiced.

Mrs Bennet, Mary and Collins are the butts of Austen's social comedy, but here it is laced with the pain of Elizabeth's embarrassment. It is difficult to know how to react to these complex circumstances, so typical of Austen, who refuses to sentimentalise family life: our heroine's mother is stupid and offensive; three of her sisters are boring or vacuous; her cousin is a monster of conceited self-importance. Can the reader take pleasure in the garishness of the occasion as Mr Bennet does? Do we thereby share some of Miss Bingley's snobbery and contempt, and Darcy's 'hauteur'? How does the comedy conflict with our sympathies for Elizabeth?

CHAPTER 19    **Mr Collins proposes to Elizabeth. She refuses him repeatedly. He insists on not believing her**

Mr Collins decides the moment for his proposal has arrived. He receives Mrs Bennet's approval. Elizabeth is left alone with Collins. He explains that it is his religious duty to marry and furthermore Lady Catherine has advised him to do so. A marriage between them would smooth over his inheriting Longbourn. Generously, he is prepared to ignore her lack of money. Elizabeth refuses him but he is determined to see her behaviour as a form of modesty or flirtatiousness, 'the usual practice of elegant females'.

Mr Collins's speech is stilted, pompous and governed by an overweening egotism. His prolix style leads him to break down his speech into numbered points: 'firstly ... secondly ... thirdly', which are unsuitable in a proposal of marriage. Elizabeth nearly laughs at the idea that this business plan has to be presented before he allows his feelings to run away on the subject of the companion that he has chosen for his future life. He shows that he has not considered her views or feelings, so certain is he of the generosity of his offer. The scene is richly comic, but harsh realities underlie the situation. Collins reminds Elizabeth that since she has so little money to her name, she may never receive another offer of marriage. The economic realities of wedlock appear in their most unattractive light.

CHAPTER 20    Mr Collins withdraws his proposal

Mrs Bennet congratulates Collins. He then tells of his interview with Elizabeth. Mrs Bennet enlists the support of Mr Bennet, and they confront Elizabeth. Her father forbids her to marry Collins. Mrs Bennet berates her wayward daughter. Collins withdraws his proposal.

The dilemma in which her father places Elizabeth – that she will lose the affection of her mother if she refuses Collins, but his affection if she accepts – is not really a dilemma at all, as he knows his wife and daughter well enough to be certain of the outcome. Austen provides a variety of perspectives on the farcical confusion, without any direct comment. For Lydia, it is 'such fun'. Mrs Bennet is locked in her absurd and self-pitiful garrulity: 'Nobody can tell what I suffer!' Mr Bennet dominates the domestic melodrama with his usual **ironic** detachment. We may wonder if his attitude borders on the facetious: though he supports Elizabeth's (and the reader's) view of Collins, he seems interested chiefly in concluding the situation with a witticism and getting everyone out of his study. Is he another egotist, like Mr Collins and Mrs Bennet? The chapter concludes with Collins's withdrawal: it is long-winded, sententious, grotesquely self-centred, a **parody** of male egocentricity.

As in the preceding chapters, Charlotte Lucas is in the background of this fracas, ready to act in ways that contrast unexpectedly with Elizabeth's decisive views.

CHAPTER 21    **Wickham explains his absence from the ball. The Bingleys leave Netherfield. Jane and Elizabeth discuss the news**

Collins is silent and resentful. He talks to Charlotte Lucas, for which Elizabeth is grateful. Mrs Bennet is still very angry with her daughter. The girls walk to Meryton and meet Wickham. He confesses to Elizabeth that he stayed away from the ball to avoid being in the same room as Darcy. Elizabeth is pleased by his attentions.

A letter arrives from Netherfield. Jane is clearly upset by the contents. When she and Elizabeth are alone Jane reads extracts and explains its substance to Elizabeth. The whole party has left Netherfield and will not be back all winter. Miss Bingley describes Georgiana Darcy and mentions her hope that Bingley will marry her. Jane is discouraged and believes that Miss Bingley is trying to let her know that Bingley is not interested in her. Elizabeth's interpretation differs entirely. She thinks that Bingley has been whisked away because his sisters do not want him to marry Jane.

In their opposed readings of the letter Elizabeth and Jane present a model for reading that resembles how we too should examine the events of the novel: every detail is scrutinised in order to infer meaning and motive, yet the text itself remains ambiguous and inscrutable. There is nothing that can lend certainty to either mutually exclusive view; all is possible, and only future events will show which of them, if either, was right in their surmise. For once Elizabeth's view is the more optimistic about the constancy of Bingley's feelings, even though she sees the letter as an ill-intentioned sisterly ploy, while Jane sees things at their worst in the long term, viewing the letter as a friendly warning.

CHAPTER 22    **Mr Collins proposes to Charlotte and is accepted.
She breaks the news to Elizabeth**

The Bennets dine with the Lucases and, once again, Charlotte occupies herself with Collins. Elizabeth thanks her. The next day Collins proposes to Charlotte. She accepts him. The Lucases are delighted, and start to speculate about Mr Bennet's death, when their daughter will take possession of Longbourn. Charlotte is pleased at the prospect of being married although she knows that her future husband is neither 'sensible nor agreeable'. She is only worried about the effect of the news on Elizabeth, but visits Elizabeth to tell her. Elizabeth is not surprised that Collins has made two proposals in three days, but she is astonished that Charlotte has accepted him. She cannot imagine that Charlotte will ever be happy.

Austen's description of Collins's proposal to Charlotte is highly **ironic**, even acidic, almost expressing hatred. (For further discussion of this, see Narrative Techniques: Irony.)

This chapter reveals the chilling version of marriage that is so very different to a union based on 'true affection' (Chapter 6). Charlotte has appraised her own situation and decides that marriage is 'the only honourable provision for well-educated young women of small fortune, and however uncertain of giving happiness, must be their pleasantest preservative from want'. Elizabeth is profoundly surprised, even shocked at her friend's mercenary decision. Her first reaction on hearing the news is that it is 'impossible'.

The reader, thanks to authorial hints and irony, has expected Collins to propose to Charlotte, and knows Charlotte's cynical views. Yet Elizabeth, for all her astuteness of observation and interest in drawing 'character', has entirely mistaken her best friend's nature. The irony is directed against her. What else can she be wrong about?

CHAPTER 23    **Charlotte's engagement is made public. Bingley stays in London**

Sir William Lucas visits in order to announce his daughter's engagement. Mrs Bennet and Lydia start by refusing to believe him. Mrs Bennet is

outraged and even more angry with Elizabeth. The friendship between
Charlotte and Elizabeth is altered. Collins writes to invite himself for
another visit, causing Mrs Bennet much displeasure.

Caroline Bingley has not replied to Jane's letter. Elizabeth worries
that his sisters will be successful in preventing Bingley from meeting Jane.
Mrs Bennet cannot bear to hear anything concerning Charlotte Lucas
though her continual talk about Bingley causes Jane great distress.

Things are going badly for the Bennet family, especially Mrs
Bennet, whose marriage plans for her daughters are falling apart.
Her distress is summed up in the lists of her muddled and
conflicting arguments. Mr Bennet takes refuge in the philosophical
reflection that 'Charlotte Lucas, whom he had been used to think
tolerably sensible, was as foolish as his wife, and more foolish than
his daughter!' The comedy is undermined or controlled by the
serious readjustments that Elizabeth has to make in relation to her
opinion of Charlotte, whom she feels she has lost as a friend, and
the mounting anxiety about Bingley's failure to return.

CHAPTER 24    Jane resolves to put Bingley behind her. Wickham
visits often

The much-awaited letter from Miss Bingley arrives. They will definitely
not return to Netherfield all winter. Bingley is staying in Darcy's home.
Darcy's sister's merits are praised, with the implication that Bingley will
marry her. Jane is determined to forget her attachment to Bingley, since
she is sure that she was mistaken in imagining that he admired her.
Elizabeth believes that he likes Jane as much as ever, but that he has
yielded to the wills of his sisters and Darcy.

Mr Wickham is often in the Longbourn household. He has told
many people of his suffering at the hands of Darcy. Jane is the only one
ever to defend Darcy.

As in Chapter 4, the differences in temperament between Jane and
Elizabeth are contrasted. Previously the opinions of Elizabeth have
been supported by Austen's depiction of events. Here, Jane's
rational reaction to Charlotte's marriage appears to be more
justified than Elizabeth's incredulity, given the economic realities of
women's lives at the time were such as to make the match 'eligible'

in all senses bar the emotional. Elizabeth's belief in love as a necessity for marriage is at odds with the novel's insistence on the importance of money.

Mr Bennet's **ironies** may suggest that he knows something about Wickham of which Elizabeth is ignorant. Is he warning Elizabeth by his comment, whose partiality for Wickham he has noticed, or is he just enjoying the free play of his irony?

CHAPTER 25    **Mr and Mrs Gardiner visit. Jane returns to London with them**

Mr Collins returns to Hunsford after planning an early wedding. Mrs Bennet's brother, Mr Gardiner and his wife come to visit. Mrs Gardiner is a particular friend of the two eldest Bennet girls. Mrs Gardiner talks to Elizabeth about Jane and Bingley. She suggests that Jane return to London with her. They do not imagine that Bingley will be allowed to visit Jane. The Gardiners stay a week. Mrs Gardiner observes Elizabeth and Wickham. Mrs Gardiner was originally from Derbyshire and is familiar with Pemberley, Darcy's estate. She enjoys discussing Derbyshire with Wickham.

Mrs Bennet's vapid nature is conveyed perfectly by her switch from discussing the serious events of her daughter's aborted engagements with the latest fashions: 'I am very glad to hear what you tell us, of long sleeves'. Mrs Gardiner is a very different character and represents the mother that Elizabeth should have had. She takes over as Elizabeth's interlocutor, furthering the debates about love and money that were initiated in conversations with Charlotte (Chapter 6).

CHAPTER 26    **Mrs Gardiner reminds Elizabeth how ill-advised a match with Wickham would be. Charlotte gets married. Jane has been snubbed by the Bingleys in London. Wickham courts an heiress**

Mrs Gardiner, having observed Elizabeth's preferential treatment of Wickham, tries to dissuade her from the relationship. She reminds Elizabeth that Wickham is not suitable for her financially or socially.

Elizabeth promises to do her best, although she does not promise not to fall in love with him. On the day before her wedding to Mr Collins Charlotte invites Elizabeth to visit her in Hunsford. The wedding takes place and Charlotte and Elizabeth become correspondents. Charlotte writes of her new home and husband with reserve and discretion. Jane also writes to Elizabeth from London, informing her that Caroline Bingley has not visited her. In her second letter, Jane writes that she has been to call on Miss Bingley but saw neither her brother nor Miss Darcy. A month later Miss Bingley returns the visit, but her behaviour to Jane is much altered. In her letter Jane acknowledges that Elizabeth was correct in her judgement of Bingley's sisters. It would appear that Bingley intends to stop leasing Netherfield. Elizabeth writes to her aunt, Mrs Gardiner, to tell her that Wickham's attentions have ceased. He is now the admirer of a certain Miss King, who has recently inherited ten thousand pounds:

> In her debate with her aunt about Wickham, her views on Jane's disappointments in London, and her response to changed affections, this chapter provides excellent examples of Elizabeth's unromantic (even cynical) wit, and pragmatic views of love, relationships and money. She is unsurprised by Caroline Bingley's mendacious behaviour, and she is able to smile at Wickham's courting someone richer than herself. Using **free indirect speech**, the narrator follows Elizabeth's thought patterns, with a pun on 'fortune', meaning both luck and financial advantage: 'she would have been his only choice, if fortune had permitted it.' For further discussion on this chapter see Textual Analysis: Text 2.

CHAPTER 27   **It is March and Elizabeth sets off to stay with Charlotte Collins, visiting Jane on the way. She agrees to a future trip with her aunt and uncle**

January and February pass by. Elizabeth is looking forward to her visit to Hunsford. She is travelling with Sir William Lucas and his daughter, Maria (both 'empty-headed'), and they plan to visit Jane on the way. She says good-bye to Wickham and is left feeling as if they will always agree and that he will always half admire her. In London Mrs Gardiner tells Elizabeth that Jane has been quite unhappy.

They discuss Wickham's new attachment to Miss King and Elizabeth speaks **ironically** of men and love. Her aunt warns her against sounding so bitter. She proposes that Elizabeth join them for a trip to the Lake District. Elizabeth is overjoyed at the prospect and accepts immediately.

The opening of this chapter is marked by narratorial comments on the dreariness of life at Longbourn. Even a visit to Mr Collins begins to seem attractive. Mr Bennet's indolent affection for Elizabeth is summed up in a single ironical sentence. He is roused by his pain at her going away to ask her to write to him, 'and almost promised to answer her letter'.

Elizabeth has the satisfaction of teasing her aunt about Wickham: 'what is the difference in matrimonial affairs, between the mercenary and the prudent motive? Where does discretion end, and avarice begin?' This discussion forms part of the debate that runs throughout the book about the role of money in romance and marriage. Elizabeth claims to be heartily sick of the whole business: 'What are men to rocks and mountains?'

CHAPTER 28    **Elizabeth arrives. They are all invited to Rosings for dinner**

Elizabeth, Sir William and Maria arrive at the Parsonage. Charlotte is pleased to see her friend, and Mr Collins is as formal and pompous as ever. Mr Collins shows them his house and grounds and prepares the guests for the honour of meeting Lady Catherine. News of Hertfordshire is exchanged. Miss De Bourgh passes by the Parsonage in her carriage and invites everyone to dine at Rosings the following evening. Elizabeth takes cruel pleasure in finding Miss De Bourgh 'sickly and cross', and therefore a fitting wife for Darcy.

Austen often shows Elizabeth's thoughts turning strangely swiftly to Darcy: is her particular detestation akin to attraction? In Chapter 16, Elizabeth, on hearing that Darcy is destined to marry Miss De Bourgh, thinks of Miss Bingley's thwarted hopes (see also Chapter 30, Chapter 31). Darcy's future wife often springs to mind, though any thought of herself in this role is denied. In Chapter 8, she is fascinated by the description of Pemberley, and puts down her book in order to be able to listen. All these are hints that **foreshadow** future events.

Most of this chapter is concerned with reviving the comic description of Mr Collins through his pride in his 'humble abode', his garden, and his noble neighbour. Sir William and Maria Lucas make good foils for his artless self-importance. Elizabeth's curiosity as to how her friend Charlotte copes with this animates her view of the situation, and she is rather impressed by her arrangements. Elizabeth's **ironical** comments about the De Bourghs are made only for her own pleasure.

CHAPTER 29    **Dinner at Rosings. Lady Catherine grills Elizabeth**

Mr Collins is overjoyed to have such a good example of Lady Catherine's munificence. He prepares his guests for the grandeur of Rosings, and reassures Elizabeth that her best clothes will be sufficient to preserve differences in rank. They arrive at Rosings. Sir William and Maria are overawed but Elizabeth feels equal to the experience. They eat a good dinner. Mr Collins carves. Lady Catherine is arrogant, self-important, overbearing and opinionated. When the women find themselves alone, she inquires into every aspect of Charlotte's housekeeping. She quizzes Elizabeth about her family and origins and is shocked to hear that the five Bennet girls were brought up without a governess. She asks how many of Elizabeth's sisters are 'out' and demands to know her age. Elizabeth dislikes her 'dignified impertinence' but answers her with 'composure'. After cards a carriage is ordered to take the party home. Elizabeth speaks as favourably as she can of the evening to please Charlotte.

> Lady Catherine is extremely rude in presuming to comment so freely on the defections of Elizabeth's upbringing, but the novel's events suggest that there may be something in her views; certainly we know that Elizabeth herself feels her young sisters are lacking in either self-discipline or parental control. Lady Catherine also has views on the entail with which Mrs Bennet would sympathise: her family estate was not entailed from the female line, and so she and her daughter are financially independent.

CHAPTER 29 continued

Lady Catherine de Bourgh is one of the great comic creations of the novel. She is an appalling snob, utterly complacent in her sense of her own exalted status and the absolute rightness of all her opinions on all subjects. Mr Collins makes an admirable acolyte, with Sir William and Maria following his lead; Elizabeth and the narrator see her for the egocentric monster she is, and Elizabeth is on the verge of meeting Lady Catherine's rudeness like for like.

CHAPTER 30    **Sir William goes home. Two weeks pass. Darcy and Colonel Fitzwilliam arrive**

Sir William stays for a week and is convinced of Charlotte's good fortune in husband and neighbours. Elizabeth notes that Charlotte has wisely arranged the rooms of the house so as not to be perpetually in the company of her husband. Most days involve a visit to Rosings, and occasionally Lady Catherine returns the courtesy. They dine twice a week at Rosings. Elizabeth is pleased to be with Charlotte and is often outdoors. Two weeks pass. It is nearly Easter and Darcy is expected at Rosings. He arrives, accompanied by Colonel Fitzwilliam, another nephew of Lady Catherine. Mr Collins goes to pay his respects and the gentlemen accompany him to the Parsonage. Elizabeth curtseys to Darcy but is silent. Darcy finally asks her about her family. She tells him that Jane has been in London and asks him if he has seen her. He seems embarrassed and replies in the negative.

Narratorial summary, in which events are seen from Elizabeth's point of view, occasionally illuminated by a fragment of direct speech, characterises this chapter. There is some finely balanced **irony** at the expense of Lady Catherine: 'whenever the cottagers were disposed to be quarrelsome, discontented, or too poor, she sallied forth into the village to settle their differences, silence their complaints, and scold them into harmony and plenty'.

CHAPTER 31    **The Parsonage party are invited to Rosings. Elizabeth talks to Colonel Fitzwilliam and Darcy**

A week after the arrival of Darcy and Colonel Fitzwilliam the Parsonage party are asked to visit Rosings after church. Lady Catherine talks mostly to her nephews, especially Darcy. Colonel Fitzwilliam is glad to see the guests. He and Elizabeth talk so much and with such animation that both Lady Catherine and Darcy notice them. Lady Catherine interrupts their conversation with her views on music, on which she claims to be an expert, though she cannot play herself. She offers her advice freely on the subject, stressing the necessity to practise. Colonel Fitzwilliam persuades Elizabeth to play. Lady Catherine talks through her performance, but Darcy seems to take an unusual interest in Elizabeth's playing and her face. They have a teasing conversation. Elizabeth reminds Darcy of not having asked her to dance in Hertfordshire. Colonel Fitzwilliam joins in the teasing. Elizabeth and Darcy assess each other's characters using the extended metaphor of practising at the piano. Lady Catherine interrupts with more advice. Elizabeth is puzzled by Darcy's attention to herself, but cattily pleased to note no special feeling between him and his cousin Miss De Bourgh.

> This chapter advances the teasing, conversational sparring between Darcy and Elizabeth, at which she is an expert. Darcy comments rather woodenly on her ironic powers; he is by contrast inadequate and defensive, but not apparently unhappy to be the butt of her wit. His pride is dissolving. Elizabeth even seems to wonder at the nature of his attentions but 'could not discern any symptom of love'. Most readers will have guessed by now that the novel's central relationship is between the two of them, and will be wondering how pride and prejudice will be overcome, or not. Lady Catherine continues to reveal her boorish ill manners and hypocritical stupidity: she is pride and prejudice personified.

CHAPTER 32    **Darcy pays Elizabeth a solo visit. He often comes to the Parsonage. Charlotte wonders why**

Elizabeth is at home alone and is visited by Darcy, 'and Darcy only'. There is an awkward silence. She asks him about the hurried way in which he and the Bingleys left Netherfield in November. He confirms Jane's news (Chapter 26) that Bingley does not intend to spend much time at Netherfield in the future, and adds that he would sell if he received an offer. They exchange barbed pleasantries about Lady Catherine's kindness and the Collins's happiness and discuss the relativity of distance; he thinks fifty miles as nearby, she does not. Puzzlingly he remarks that she cannot have lived all her life at Longbourn. Further visits from Darcy and Colonel Fitzwilliam lead Elizabeth to compare the latter to her former admirer Wickham, and Charlotte to wonder if the former can be in love with Elizabeth. Darcy is mostly silent on these visits, but looks at her a lot, though whether with love and admiration, or merely absentmindedness is not clear. Charlotte is sure that Elizabeth would accept Darcy 'could she suppose him to be in her power'. Comparing Fitzwilliam and Darcy as future husbands for her friend, she has the practical thought that Darcy is the one with 'patronage in the church'.

> The reader needs to study Darcy's strange comments in this chapter, to evaluate what may be going on is his mind: is he clumsily suggesting that Elizabeth's sophistication could not have been acquired in her home? This is not much of a compliment, as it reveals his prejudice against her family. Elizabeth does not seem to consider the implications of his remark. Charlotte's reflections on how quickly Elizabeth might fall for Darcy, and which prospective husband for her friend would best serve herself, adds to the novel's pragmatic consideration of marriage in terms of power and money. This may be perceived, in Charlotte and in the narrator, as either engagingly honest or distastefully unromantic.

CHAPTER 33   **Elizabeth keeps on meeting Darcy while she is walking. Colonel Fitzwilliam tells her that Darcy has prevented a friend from an ill-advised marriage. Elizabeth can only think of Bingley and Jane. She does not go to Rosings that evening**

Elizabeth meets Darcy when she is walking in the park. At their third meeting he seems to be asking her some odd questions. He implies that during some future visit she will stay at Rosings. Elizabeth thinks that he must be referring to a possible match between herself and Colonel Fitzwilliam, and is distressed by the implication.

She is walking in the park again, reading Jane's old letters to her, when she meets Colonel Fitzwilliam. He tells her that Darcy keeps delaying their departure. They talk about money, and Elizabeth is embarrassed when Colonel Fitzwilliam states that he could not marry 'without some attention to money'. She turns the conversation to a humorous evaluation of the price for a prospective wife for a man in his position. She learns that Fitzwilliam is a joint guardian with Darcy of Georgiana Darcy. Elizabeth infers that there has been some trouble with her, and changes the subject to speak of the Bingleys. Colonel Fitzwilliam tells her, in order to illustrate the very great friendship existing between Darcy and Bingley, that the former had dissuaded him from an 'imprudent marriage' to a woman against whom there were 'very strong objections'. Elizabeth immediately thinks of Jane and Bingley and is indignant and angry. Later she speculates about the objections, which she deems snobbish prejudice against her relatives, mere lawyers; her confidence wanes a little when she remembers her mother's 'want of sense'. She cries, gets a headache, and does not go to Rosings that evening.

The reader alert to Darcy's strangled feelings for Elizabeth will enjoy the **irony** of Elizabeth's blithe misreading of his behaviour in the park, and groan at Fitzwilliam's revelations about Darcy's role in separating Jane and Bingley, which is obviously going to obstruct or prevent the working out of their relationship.

In Chapter 35 we discover that Darcy is much more struck by Elizabeth's relations' 'want of propriety' than by their position in society. Elizabeth misjudges him in this chapter, ascribing to him more pride and snobbishness than he actually possesses. She too is prejudiced against him.

Later in the novel (Chapters 35, 41) both Darcy and Mr Bennet claim that the elder Bennet girls can escape the restrictions and embarrassments of their family purely by means of their own meritorious behaviour. Class division, and the possible crossing of social boundaries that seem insurmountable is one given **theme** of *Pride and Prejudice.* But here Elizabeth believes that Darcy's snobbery has prevailed so as to squash Jane's hopes of marriage with Bingley.

CHAPTER 34    Darcy proposes to Elizabeth and is refused

Nursing her anger at Darcy's interference, Elizabeth re-examines all the letters that Jane has sent her. They lack 'cheerfulness'. She consoles herself with the fact that Darcy is due to leave within two days and that within a fortnight she will see Jane again in London. She will be sorry to see Colonel Fitzwilliam leave but she knows from their discussion of money that he could never marry her. She is surprised to hear the doorbell, and amazed to see Darcy enter the room.

He tells her that he loves her. She is silent. He tells her of his love, and, in doing so, dwells on the problem posed by her inferiority. He seems sure that she will accept him. Elizabeth would have refused him even had his request been made differently. But she is offended by his lack of tact, and treats him without much compassion. When he realises that she is rejecting him, Darcy asks her why she is so uncivil about it. Elizabeth charges him with ruining Jane's happiness, and tells him that she has disliked him since she heard about how he treated Wickham. He replies by suggesting that she might have overlooked these factors if he had not offended her by mentioning the very real social and financial obstacles to their match. Elizabeth, enraged, tells him that she would never have accepted him, however he had asked her and accuses him of not behaving in a gentlemanlike manner. She adds that after knowing him for a month, 'I felt that you were the last man in the world whom I could ever be prevailed on to marry'. Darcy leaves the room. Elizabeth cries. She is flattered that he should have asked her, but curses his 'abominable pride'. She goes to her room in order not to have to meet Charlotte.

> Who is more in the wrong in this melodramatic scene? Darcy's bumbling explanations of what he had to overcome on order to allow himself to court Elizabeth, his strong sense of his own superior position in society, and his easy assumption that she will accept his hand, are all unsympathetic aspects of his proposal. But events prove that Elizabeth is rash to have trusted Wickham's account of Darcy, and her rejection of the proposal is spiced with some self-righteous anger. Her manner of putting him down is consonant with Austen's creation of her as a feisty, witty and self-confident young woman.

Darcy's proposal appears at a strategic point, midway through the novel. From this point on, there are far fewer social ceremonies (balls, dinners, dances) and, instead, Elizabeth is to spend more time in reflection. Maturation of private judgement takes the place of witty public display.

CHAPTER 35    **Elizabeth is given a letter by Darcy. He explains his conduct with Bingley and Wickham**

Elizabeth goes for a walk. She meets Darcy who hands her a letter. In it he explains his belief that Jane was 'indifferent' to Bingley. He describes the problems posed by an association with the Bennet family: Mrs Bennet's low connections, but more the 'total lack of propriety so frequently, so almost uniformly betrayed by herself, your three younger sisters, and occasionally even by your father'. The behaviour of all at the ball at Netherfield convinces him of the undesirability of the match. Thereafter, Darcy, encouraged by Bingley's sisters, joined Bingley in London and dissuaded him from marriage. He admits that he knew that Jane was in London and that he hid this knowledge from Bingley. He describes Wickham's upbringing and the close relationship that existed between the late Darcy and his godson. Darcy senior paid for Wickham to go to Cambridge University and hoped to provide him with a career in the church. Darcy junior had never been as impressed with Wickham as his father was. He had the task of promoting Wickham's career and giving him a living and a legacy of a thousand pounds. Some six months later Wickham wrote to Darcy to inform him that he had no intention of following a career in the church. Darcy gave him the thousand pounds. Wickham renounced his claim to the living and was given an immediate pay-off of three thousand pounds. Darcy and Wickham heard nothing of each other for three years. Wickham wrote to ask for the church living that he had refused. Darcy refused. Finally during the preceding summer Wickham tried to elope with Miss Darcy and was only just prevented by the intervention of Darcy. Darcy closes his letter to Elizabeth with an assurance of the truth of his account.

> *Pride and Prejudice* is peppered with letters: forty-four in all are cited, either in full, like Darcy's here, or fragments are quoted or mentioned. Jane Austen was herself a prolific writer of lively and

entertaining letters. **Epistolary novels** were common reading material of the day.

In letters, as opposed to conversation, things can be written and explained that could never be spoken in a social situation. Letters can be studied and reread and the attitudes to the writer can mature and change. Darcy comments that he was not sufficiently 'master' of himself to reveal in conversation what he has put in the letter. He asserts that his 'character required it to be written and read'. Darcy may not be much of a conversationalist, but he writes a strong and intelligent letter, which is something of a bombshell so far as Elizabeth is concerned. In the next chapter we see what effect the process of reading and digesting his argument has on her.

CHAPTER 36    **Elizabeth reads and rereads the letter and is ashamed of her prejudice. Darcy and Colonel Fitzwilliam leave Rosings**

On first reading of the letter, convinced as she is of Darcy's guilt, Elizabeth is angered by his reference to her family and incredulous about his account of Wickham's behaviour. She rereads the letter and realises that Darcy may be entirely blameless in the affair. She recalls that she had no knowledge of Wickham before being introduced to him and recognises the inappropriate way he told her his personal history on their second meeting. She remembers that Wickham chose to avoid Darcy at the Netherfield ball, and that, after Bingley and Darcy had left the county, Wickham did not scruple to inform everybody of his situation. She now sees Wickham's attentions to Miss King in a different light and questions the motives behind Wickham's attentions to herself. Elizabeth is ashamed and curses her prejudice. She reads again Darcy's account of Jane and Bingley and realises that he could well have mistaken her reserve for want of feeling. She remembers the behaviour of the Bennets at the Netherfield ball (Chapter 18) and acknowledges the justice in his comments on her family. She realises that she has been 'partial, prejudiced, absurd'. She feels justly humiliated.

On her return to the Parsonage she discovers that Darcy and Fitzwilliam have both visited to pay their respects before leaving Kent.

This chapter contains the second mention of the word 'prejudice'. The first is in Chapter 18, when Elizabeth, referring indirectly to Wickham, asks Darcy if he ever allows himself to be 'blinded by prejudice'. It is relevant that the word, to which the reader is sensitised by the novel's title, should reappear in relation to Wickham's character. This chapter is central to the movement of the novel since it marks the turnaround in Elizabeth's opinion.

In this description of Elizabeth's appraisal of the letter and its material Austen provides us with a model for reading. To begin with, we read superficially and see only what we want, but rereading and rereading can result in a complete shift in all our perspectives. In *Emma* (1816) Austen tricks her characters and the reader into a number of wrong interpretations of events; on rereading we can see that all the clues were there for the sharp-eyed. *Pride and Prejudice* to a lesser degree plays this trick on the reader. Here Elizabeth is forced to revise her attitudes and understanding; up till now, she has been misreading the situation. The reader also has to share this process of re-interpretation and realignment, going over the events of the novel to see if, like Elizabeth, they have lacked the moral scrupulosity to see through Wickham, to judge Darcy fairly, to comprehend how much the Bennet family are lacking in propriety. Austen wants us also to struggle with these new implications.

CHAPTER 37    **Elizabeth studies the letter and is unhappy. She and Maria Lucas prepare to leave for London**

Lady Catherine summons Mr and Mrs Collins and their guests to Rosings. She tells Elizabeth that she should stay longer at the Parsonage. Elizabeth tells her that she must go, and the particulars of the journey are discussed. When she is alone she studies Darcy's letter and has soon learnt it by heart. She does not regret having rejected him, but she is ashamed of the way in which she did it, and now feels some compassion for him. She is embarrassed by 'the unhappy defects of her family', in particular the propensity of Catherine and Lydia to flirt with officers, with their mother's encouragement. Above all Elizabeth is unhappy that 'the folly and indecorum of her own family' should have cost Jane her chance of happiness.

The narrator shows how completely Elizabeth has come to believe in Darcy's letter, and what misery this brings her. Lady Catherine's pomposity is a comic foil to this new seriousness.

CHAPTER 38    **Elizabeth and Maria leave. They arrive at the Gardiner's in London**

Mr Collins thanks Elizabeth for her visit with elaborate and long-winded formality, reminding her of the kindness she has received in the superior society of Lady Catherine. He boasts about the success of his marriage. Elizabeth is truly sorry to leave Charlotte.

Elizabeth and Maria arrive at Mrs Gardiner's house. Jane looks well. Elizabeth resolves not to tell her of Darcy's disclosures until they are returned to Longbourn. She decides that she will not tell Jane anything concerning Bingley.

So elaborate are Mr Collins's compliments that Austen runs the risk of boring the reader. The contrast between his own self-satisfaction and Elizabeth's short replies is typical of this chapter, which is marked by the gulf between Elizabeth's private feelings and the trivial public conversation in which she has to participate.

CHAPTER 39    **Elizabeth, Maria and Jane set off for Hertfordshire. They are met by Lydia and Kitty**

It is the second week of May. Elizabeth, Maria and Jane travel back to Longbourn and are met by Kitty and Lydia, who have ordered a meal at an inn for them all, but are unable to pay for it because they have spent their money on hats. Lydia tells them that the regiment are leaving the area in a fortnight's time and will be encamped at Brighton for the summer. Miss King has moved away and Lydia pronounces that Wickham is 'safe.' Lydia talks for the entirety of the journey home. She asks her sisters if they have 'had any flirting' and regales them with tales of practical jokes and officers. Wickham is mentioned frequently.

Mrs Bennet is pleased to see her daughters, and Mr Bennet stirs himself so far as to tell Elizabeth 'more than once' that he is glad that she has come home. Lydia dominates the lunch. She wants to walk to

Meryton that afternoon. Elizabeth opposes the plan. She has no inclination to see Wickham, and is relieved to think that he will be gone in two weeks. Mrs Bennet is pressing her husband to allow her daughters to go to Brighton for the summer.

Lydia's speech is characterised by exclamations, rhetorical questions, incomplete sentences and invocations: 'Aye', 'Lord' and 'La'. Her speech is even more wild and digressive than that of her mother. She is loud and listens to no one. But she does have a youthful and vulgar vitality that is not to be ignored. Here all Elizabeth's newly exacerbated fears about her family are confirmed. Lydia's anarchic fecklessness, the plan to stay in Brighton, and her father's refusal clearly to disallow it, all these are stark reminders of the impropriety that Darcy summed up in his letter.

CHAPTER 40     **Elizabeth tells Jane about Darcy's love and his letter. They decide not to dishonour Wickham**

Elizabeth finally tells Jane about what has occurred between her and Darcy, omitting any reference to Jane and Bingley. Jane cannot believe Wickham's 'wickedness' and is distressed on Darcy's account. The sisters discuss whether they ought to make Wickham's character publicly known and decide that since he is soon to leave they may as well keep silent. Elizabeth realises that Jane is not happy and is still very much in love with Bingley.

Mrs Bennet has given up any hope of Bingley marrying Jane. She asks Elizabeth about the Collins' and Charlotte's household management, and expresses her bitterness at the entailment which will make Mr Collins the eventual owner of Longbourn.

In this chapter Austen contrasts the two sisters by means of their reactions to the tale of Darcy's proposal and his letter. Jane is all softness and compassion at Darcy's misery, and amazement at Wickham's wickedness. In assessing her prejudiced behaviour towards Darcy, Elizabeth criticises herself, but she still prefers to filter her reaction through a mordant wit. Their discussion focuses one of the **themes** of the novel, the discrepancy between appearance and reality, as made manifest in Darcy and Wickham: 'One has all the goodness, and the other all the appearance of it'.

CHAPTER 41   **Lydia is invited to Brighton. Elizabeth advises her father not to let her go. Elizabeth meets Wickham. Lydia leaves for Brighton**

The regiment is to leave in a week's time. This makes Kitty and Lydia miserable. They still hope to go to Brighton. Elizabeth is ashamed of their behaviour and remembers Darcy's objections with understanding. Lydia is overjoyed when the wife of Colonel Forster invites her to Brighton. Kitty is peevish not to be included. Elizabeth secretly advises Mr Bennet not to allow Lydia to go. She tells him in the strongest terms that Lydia's imprudent behaviour is detrimental to them all. Mr Bennet is **ironic** and attributes her intervention to self-concern: 'What, has she frightened away some of your lovers?' When Mr Bennet sees how serious Elizabeth is he explains his belief that Colonel Forster will control Lydia and that she will be of less account in Brighton, which may do her good.

Before the departure of the regiment Elizabeth meets Wickham several times. She now finds his manners unconvincing and is displeased when he seems to be renewing his attentions to her. She tells him that she has spent time with Darcy and Colonel Fitzwilliam at Rosings. Elizabeth discreetly conveys to Wickham that she no longer shares his negative opinion of Darcy, and he is suitably anxious that his pretence has been discovered. They part with 'mutual civility, and … a mutual desire of never meeting again'. When Lydia leaves, Kitty weeps with envy.

This is a very varied chapter that contains stark opposites of behaviour and feeling. In a strange passage unlike anything else in the book, the narrator enters Lydia's 'imagination' and shows the vision of Brighton she has constructed 'with the creative eye of fancy'. Her fantasy accords with Elizabeth's description of her as 'a flirt … in the worst and meanest degree of flirtation'. But the contrast between Lydia's fevered excitement and Elizabeth's eloquent anger could not be greater. Mr Bennet starts by mocking Elizabeth, but her new seriousness causes him to lower his **ironic** defences. He expresses real admiration for Jane and Elizabeth, and shows by his explanation that he has at least given the matter of Lydia's folly some thought.

Elizabeth also shows her strength and moral purpose with Wickham, whom she now sees as affected and dishonest. He is left not quite knowing where he stands with her – does she know the truth about his past? She states that Darcy has improved by 'knowing him better'; but Wickham claims that Darcy is 'wise enough to assume … the *appearance* of what is right'. The narrator picks up the word, and comments on Wickham's continued *appearance* of 'usual cheerfulness', though he is obviously rattled. We are reminded of Jane and Elizabeth's discussion in the preceding chapter, and that appearance and reality is a **theme** examined throughout the book. Lydia's fantasy of Brighton is based also all on appearance. The underlying moral reality is presented in Elizabeth's grim view.

CHAPTER 42    **Mr Bennet's marriage is explained and Elizabeth's anxieties at his irresponsible behaviour are explored. The Lake District trip is changed to Derbyshire. The Gardiners and Elizabeth arrive at Lambton, five miles from Pemberley. They resolve to visit the estate**

The narrator explains the background to Mr Bennet's marriage. He fell in love with his wife's youth and beauty, but soon lost any love for her. He has devoted his life to reading, and finds in Mrs Bennet a source of amusement and little more. Elizabeth concedes that her father's behaviour has been irresponsible, especially so far as his daughters are concerned.

Elizabeth looks forward to her visit to the Lakes with the Gardiners, though it is sad that Jane is not able to accompany them. However Elizabeth takes a cynical solace in the fact that as the holiday plan is not quite perfect, she is less likely to be disappointed by it. Lydia writes hurried and infrequent letters.

Things begin to cheer up a month after Lydia's departure. The social life of Longbourn starts up again. Only two weeks remain before Elizabeth is due to begin her 'Northern tour'. Mrs Gardiner writes to postpone their departure and shorten the journey. The new plan is to go only as far as Derbyshire and to visit the places in which Mrs Gardiner used to live. Elizabeth is very disappointed. She cannot think of Derbyshire without thinking of Darcy and his family home at Pemberley. Finally the Gardiners arrive. Their children are left under Jane's supervision. Elizabeth and the Gardiners find themselves in the small village of Lambton, some five miles away from Pemberley. Mrs Gardiner longs to visit Pemberley. Elizabeth dreads meeting Darcy, but, after finding out that he is absent, she agrees to accompany her aunt.

> Spanning six weeks or so between Lydia's leaving and Elizabeth's summer tour, this chapter imparts general information mixed with amusing circumstantial detail. It·is odd that Austen has delayed the explanation of the unhappiness in Mr Bennet's marriage, and his refuge in the countryside, books and the ironic consolations of the 'true philosopher'. However, it follows on naturally from Elizabeth's vain attempt to advise her father, and spells out her attitude to him. She is grateful for his affection and respectful of his abilities, but has to strive to forget 'that continual breach of conjugal obligation and decorum which, in exposing his wife to the contempt of her own children, was so highly reprehensible'. The severe abstraction of this kind of commentary is sharpened by contrast with Kitty's letters.
>
> It is essential for our belief in Elizabeth's good faith that she should not be instrumental in deciding to visit Pemberley, otherwise it might look as if she has set out to capture Darcy. And so the narrator stresses how much Elizabeth really wanted to go to the Lakes, how unwilling she is to visit Pemberley, and how careful she is to ascertain that Darcy is not in residence.
>
> **petrified spars** fossils, to be collected as souvenirs

CHAPTER 43    **The Gardiners and Elizabeth visit Pemberley. Darcy appears. He treats them with surprising civility**

Elizabeth is agitated as they enter Pemberley woods and arrive at Pemberley House. She reflects 'that to be mistress of Pemberley might be something!', and cannot help wondering what it would have been like to have lived there. They are shown about the house by Mrs Reynolds, the housekeeper. She is delighted to talk about her master, Darcy. Elizabeth sees paintings of Wickham, Darcy and Miss Darcy. She is surprised to discover that Darcy is considered by his servant to be anything but proud. Mrs Reynolds claims never to have heard a cross word from him. He is kind to his tenants, to the poor and to his sister. Elizabeth is amazed.

Darcy himself appears. Elizabeth is shocked and deeply embarrassed. She thinks that Darcy will attribute her presence to the worst of motives. Darcy is confused but perfectly polite. In fact, despite what has passed between them, he is more gentle and polite than he has ever been before to Elizabeth. He leaves her and they continue the walk about the grounds, though Elizabeth can scarcely concentrate. To her further astonishment Darcy appears again and asks to be introduced to the Gardiners. Darcy is surprised to discover who they are but nonetheless invites Mr Gardiner to fish in his river. Darcy tells Elizabeth that Bingley and his sisters are about to arrive. He asks if he may introduce his sister to Elizabeth. This is a great honour, and Elizabeth is astonished for the third time. This seems proof that Darcy can feel no resentment towards her.

On the way home Elizabeth's aunt and uncle praise Darcy but Mrs Gardiner, still believing Wickham has been Darcy's victim, continues to talk about Wickham and to compare the two men. Elizabeth relates an abbreviated version of the true relationship between them. That evening Elizabeth can think of nothing else but of Darcy's kindness and his wish that she should meet his sister.

In Chapter 8, when the conversation turned to Pemberley, Elizabeth had put down her book to listen. It is clearly supposed to be a famous country house, and the narrator describes the picturesque scenery and the house that surrounds it in more exact detail and at greater length than she does any other house or park in the novel. It is rather an abstract and frigid description (there are no **metaphors** to make it come alive), but it is a coherent and whole picture. The way it merges with the natural features without any appearance of artificiality is in line with contemporary aesthetics of the country house. It may also offer an implicit key to Darcy's character: there is more robust naturalness in him than artifice.

CHAPTER 43 continued

The visit to Pemberley is seen through Elizabeth's perceptions. She is very curious to see the house, and allows herself almost to feel regret that she is not its mistress. She is surprised and impressed by the housekeeper's love for her master: 'she longed to hear more'. This is flatly opposite to her own convictions as to his arrogance and bad temper.

After Darcy's appearance she is flustered and embarrassed – she knows she should not be found visiting the house of a man whose offer of marriage she has rebuffed – but she still manages to watch him to see how he reacts. She cannot understand why he is being so polite and her curiosity is extreme. During this chapter her feelings towards Darcy start to change. Pemberley forces Elizabeth to start imagining what kind of person Darcy really is. Only a few shreds of her prejudice remain.

The reader feels a certain amusement in seeing Elizabeth undergo her emotional *volte-face*. This comedy is underlined by Elizabeth's desire to keep the whole business a secret from her aunt and uncle. The **dramatic irony** caused by Elizabeth's keeping her relationship with Darcy a secret remains till almost the novel's end.

CHAPTER 44   **Miss Darcy and Bingley visit the Gardiners**

Miss Darcy comes to visit on the very day that she has arrived at Pemberley. Elizabeth sees the Darcy carriage from the window of the inn at Lambton, and warns her aunt and uncle of the impending visit. The Gardiners begin to imagine that Darcy may be partial to their niece. Elizabeth is very agitated and keen to please Miss Darcy.

Miss Darcy arrives and Elizabeth realises that she is not proud but only very shy. She is sixteen and 'womanly and graceful'. Bingley joins them and Elizabeth observes him carefully. Mr and Mrs Gardiner are also fascinated by their guests, and are becoming sure that Darcy is in love with Elizabeth. She believes from some of his looks and enquiries that Bingley may be still interested in Jane.

Darcy continues to be as pleasant as on the preceding day, and Elizabeth wonders at his kindness towards her aunt and uncle, whose company he would formerly have shunned. Darcy asks his sister to invite the Gardiners and Elizabeth to Pemberley for dinner in two days' time.

Wickham is not popular in Lambton. Darcy paid off Wickham's debts when he left the area.

Elizabeth lies awake and tries to decide how she feels about Darcy. She realises that she feels respect, esteem and gratitude towards him. She thinks that he is probably still in love with her, and wonders whether she should try to make him renew his addresses, which she thinks she has the 'power' to do. The next day promises a visit to Pemberley. Mrs Gardiner and Elizabeth have decided to repay Miss Darcy's courtesy by returning their visit with similar promptness.

The focus shifts occasionally away from Elizabeth to the Gardiners. From watching her and Darcy they have quickly arrived at 'the full conviction that one of them at least knew what it was to love. Of the lady's sensations they remained a little in doubt'. Most of the chapter, however, deals with Elizabeth's consciousness in the light of Darcy's behaviour. Elizabeth spends as much time watching Bingley for signs of his continued love for Jane as she does keeping an eye on Darcy. At night, however, she thinks over the day's events and realises that she is grateful to him for forgiving her for 'their last lively scene in Hunsford'. Such a change in him can only be attributed to 'love, ardent love'. Her *volte-face* continues.

The discovery that Georgiana is not proud but shy provides Elizabeth with another clue to Darcy's character. Embarrassment and shyness colour all their encounters from now until Darcy proposes again. They discuss this in Chapter 60.

CHAPTER 45    **Mrs Gardiner and Elizabeth visit Pemberley. Miss Bingley is spiteful**

Mrs Gardiner and Elizabeth arrive at Pemberley and are received by Miss Darcy. The Bingley sisters barely acknowledge them. Elizabeth waits for Darcy's appearance with apprehension. Elizabeth realises that everyone is watching how Darcy and herself will behave, and so she makes a concentrated effort to appear 'easy and unembarrassed'. Miss Bingley is jealous of Elizabeth, and is irritated to see that Darcy is doing everything to make his sister and Elizabeth acquainted. By asking Elizabeth about the departure of the regiment from Meryton she alludes to Elizabeth's interest in Wickham. But Miss Bingley is unaware of Miss

Darcy's near elopement with Wickham, and unintentionally causes embarrassment to Darcy and his sister. Clearly only Elizabeth shares this secret.

When Elizabeth and Mrs Gardiner leave, Miss Bingley immediately criticises Elizabeth's 'person, behaviour, dress'. Georgiana will not join her in these opinions. Miss Bingley remarks to Darcy on the deterioration in Elizabeth's looks and reminds him of his first opinion of Elizabeth at Netherfield: '*She* a beauty! — I should as soon as call her mother a wit!'. Darcy is finally stung into telling her that he considers Elizabeth to be 'one of the handsomest women of my acquaintance'.

Mrs Gardiner and Elizabeth discuss the visit but neither touch on the topics that really interest them.

The jealous malice of Caroline Bingley and her interesting inability to control herself runs throughout this scene. She has nothing to gain from her rudeness about Elizabeth, which she should see will only annoy Darcy. Yet she is unable to check herself from goading him till she hears exactly the praise of Elizabeth that is most hurtful to her. Such malice combined with curiosity is a particular public trial to Elizabeth, and then to Darcy. Miss Bingley, like Lady Catherine later, achieves exactly the opposite of her intention. Rather than turning Darcy against Elizabeth, it brings the two of them together in the mutual knowledge of a shared secret. And then it forces Darcy to make public his admiration for Elizabeth.

CHAPTER 46     **Letters from Jane arrive. Lydia has run away with Wickham. Darcy visits and hears this news. The Gardiners and Elizabeth leave Lambton for Longbourn**

Elizabeth receives two long-awaited letters from Jane. In the first letter Jane writes that Lydia has run away to Scotland with Wickham. She is 'willing to hope the best' of the match, and believes that Wickham must be in love with Lydia since he knows that she will bring him no money.

The second letter, written a day later, conveys the family fear that Lydia and Wickham do not intend marriage, but are living in sin. Colonel Forster has tried to pursue them, but to no avail. Jane begs Elizabeth to ask Mr Gardiner if he would be so kind as to help their father in London. Just as Elizabeth sets out to find her aunt and uncle Darcy arrives. He is alarmed at how ill she looks. Darcy comforts her as well as he can, and then leaves.

Elizabeth assumes that this latest family disgrace will dispel any love that Darcy might have felt for her. She realises, however, that she could have loved him.

Lydia had never seemed particularly interested in Wickham, but Elizabeth recognises that she was ready to attach herself to anyone, and that her virtue is not to be relied upon. The Gardiners return. Elizabeth reads them the letters, and they resolve to leave immediately. After an hour they are on the road to Longbourn. Mrs Gardiner wonders whether Elizabeth has told Darcy of this catastrophe.

> This is one of the book's melodramatic centres. Several shifts of focus bring intelligence to what could have been no more than sensational. Notably, Elizabeth is torn between a generalised concern for Lydia and her family, and a specific anxiety about what effect this will have on Darcy's apparent interest in her. The disgrace Lydia has brought on the family must be just the kind of vulgarity of which he most disapproves. By a terrible **irony** of the kind Austen seems to enjoy, just at the moment when it seems all must be over with Darcy, Elizabeth discovers that she has fallen in love with him. For further discussion, see Textual Analysis: Text 3.

CHAPTER 47    **At Longbourn there is no news of Lydia. Elizabeth sees Lydia's letter. Mr Gardiner prepares to join Mr Bennet in London**

Mr Gardiner thinks that perhaps Wickham and Lydia have married in London. Elizabeth points out that Wickham will not have married Lydia since she has no money. She reflects how Lydia has been allowed to run wild during the past year. Elizabeth recalls Wickham's terrible behaviour to Darcy. We know that she is also thinking of his attempted elopement with Miss Darcy. Mrs Gardiner is puzzled at what secret information Elizabeth seems to have about Wickham. Once again Elizabeth regrets not having made public her knowledge of Wickham's true character when she returned to Meryton.

They arrive at Longbourn the next day. Nothing has been heard of

CHAPTER 47 continued

the fugitives yet. Mr Bennet is in London while Mrs Bennet does not leave her dressing room. Absurdly, she blames her husband for not letting her accompany Lydia to Brighton, and is worried about the prospect of Mr Bennet duelling with Wickham. Mr Gardiner reassures her and prepares to set off for London.

Alone at last with Jane, Elizabeth learns that Colonel Forster does not trust Wickham; he left Meryton with many debts outstanding. Elizabeth is shown Lydia's note explaining her departure. She describes the 'good joke' of breaking the news of her marriage to her family. Elizabeth is shocked, but consoled to think that it was at least Lydia's intention to marry Wickham.

The various family reactions to Lydia's disgrace are paralleled and contrasted in this chapter. Jane is optimistic and trying to see the best in everyone. The Gardiners are cautiously helpful and concerned. Mrs Bennet blames everyone but herself, and is hysterically torn between worrying what clothes Lydia will buy in London and fantasising about her husband fighting with Wickham. Mr Bennet has converted his shock into silence, and has only written one short note from London. Mary delivers a sermon on the fragility of female virtue. Elizabeth keeps her intelligence and **irony** at play, fully conscious of the worst that is likely to have happened to Lydia, but irritated by the neighbours' malicious curiosity.

CHAPTER 48    **Mr Gardiner leaves for London. Mr Collins sends a letter. Mr Bennet comes home. Still no news of the fugitives**

Mr Bennet, never a good correspondent, has not written, and Mr Gardiner, after waiting in vain for a letter, leaves for London. Mrs Gardiner stays on to help her nieces. Their other aunt, Mrs Philips, visits often. She generally brings some new tale of Wickham's 'extravagance or irregularity'. The whole of Meryton is full of stories of Wickham's debts and seductions. Mr Gardiner writes to say that they have still had no success.

A letter arrives from Mr Collins. It is pompous and self-important. He suggests that Mr Bennet disown Lydia, adding that it would be infinitely preferable had she been dead.

Mr Gardiner has been trying to trace Wickham's family or friends, but with little success. Wickham left the army in secret because he had many gambling debts, at which Jane is very shocked.

Mrs Gardiner arranges to leave with her children. She is still puzzled as to the situation between Elizabeth and Darcy. Mr Bennet returns. He accepts the blame for Lydia's behaviour, while acknowledging that his feelings of guilt and shame will 'pass away soon enough'. He tells Elizabeth that he does not begrudge her having been right about not sending Lydia to Brighton (Chapter 41). He teases Kitty by threatening to be incredibly strict with her.

In this chapter there is a further array of different reactions to the news of the family's disgrace. Mr Collins's letter is grotesquely callous, though it pretends to sympathy. The reader may wonder why Austen gives the most hypocritical and uncharitable view of the situation to a clergyman.

Austen's portrayal of Mr Bennet's behaviour at the low point of the family's misfortunes is particularly interesting. Even when admitting his responsibility for Lydia's misbehaviour to Elizabeth, he still retains an ironic detachment that the reader may choose to find either sympathetically amusing or somewhat shockingly disengaged from the grim reality of the situation.

CHAPTER 49   **Mr Gardiner writes that Lydia and Wickham have been found, but are not yet married. Mr Bennet realises that Wickham's acceptance of Lydia must have involved a large sum of money. Mrs Bennet is overjoyed that one daughter is at last to be married**

The housekeeper tells Jane and Elizabeth that an express letter has arrived from Mr Gardiner. They run to find their father, who gives them the letter to read. Lydia and Wickham have been located. They are not married. Mr Gardiner has proposed to settle £100 per year on Lydia, which works out as her share of the money she would inherit from her parents. Lydia is to be married from the Gardiner's home. Mr Bennet is reluctant to reply. He has realised that Mr Gardiner must have paid a great sum of money to persuade Wickham to marry Lydia. Mrs Bennet is overjoyed, and immediately begins to think about wedding clothes. Her

CHAPTER 49 continued

daughters explain Mr Gardiner's presumed generosity, but Mrs Bennet does not consider this of any account.

Mr Bennet shows a proper concern that he will not be able repay his brother-in-law whatever large sum must have been offered to Wickham. This is contrasted with Mrs Bennet's unreflecting delight in Lydia's prospective marriage. The superficiality of Mrs Bennet's response is compounded by her thoughtless and selfish lack of concern for her brother's generosity, which she dismisses as simply what is due from him.

Mrs Bennet is linked to Lydia by their lack of moral reflection and their shared obsession with clothes. We may recall how in Chapter 39 Lydia bought a bonnet with the money intended for the sisters' lunch. Austen uses the **motif** as a way of indicating the worst excesses of female silliness: Jane and Elizabeth in contrast seem little interested in fashion or drapery.

CHAPTER 50     **Mr Bennet approves Mr Gardiner's suggestions. Elizabeth realises that she loves Darcy. Lydia is to visit Longbourn after her wedding**

Mr Bennet wishes that he had put more effort into saving money. He and his wife had hoped to have a son in order to cut off the entail. The debt he owes to his brother-in-law, Mr Gardiner, weighs heavy upon him. Mr Bennet writes to Mr Gardiner authorising Lydia's entitlement to her share of the £5000 settled on his wife and children. He is too angry to send Lydia a message. Mrs Bennet comes down from her bedroom for the first time in two weeks. In defiance of their true financial situation, she starts thinking of the various properties in the surrounding area where the couple might live. Mr Bennet tells her that Lydia will never be allowed under his roof. He adds that he will not give her any money to finance wedding clothes or the wedding itself. Mrs Bennet is horrified and amazed.

Elizabeth begins to wish that she had never told Darcy about Lydia's disgrace. She reflects bitterly that there is very little chance of Darcy ever wanting to connect himself in any way to Wickham. She realises that she now thinks of Darcy as the perfect husband for herself.

Mr Gardiner writes once more begging Mr Bennet not to mention the matter of money again. Wickham intends to join the regular army, and is seeking a posting in the north. Wickham's debts in Brighton are to be settled. Mrs Bennet is distressed to think of her daughter being so far away. Lydia wishes to visit before she leaves, and, thanks to the efforts of Jane and Elizabeth, their father gives his permission. It is arranged that the newly-wed couple will come to Longbourn after the wedding ceremony.

Austen gives precise details of the financial arrangements. We learn that Mr Bennet will be scarcely £10 a year 'the loser' with the settlement on Lydia. His irresponsibility as a father is exemplified by the absence of financial provision for his daughters, exposing them to the realities of the marriage market. Other novels by Austen feature similar incompetent father figures, though Mr Gardiner is a model of domestic responsibility.

The contrast initiated in the last chapter between Mr Bennet's anger and anxiety (tempered by his **irony** and indolence), and Mrs Bennet's inability to grasp the financial and moral realities of Lydia's behaviour is brought to a head here. Mrs Bennet 'was more alive to the disgrace, which the want of new clothes must reflect on her daughter's nuptials, than to any sense of shame at her eloping and living with Wickham'.

Elizabeth's reflections on how she feels about Darcy are placed in heavily ironic counterpoint with the knowledge that circumstances have made it impossible for him now have any interest in her.

CHAPTER 51    **Lydia and Wickham arrive. Elizabeth discovers that Darcy was present at their wedding. She writes to Mrs Gardiner to find out more**

Lydia arrives and is the same as ever: 'untamed, unabashed, wild, noisy, and fearless'. Elizabeth, Jane and their father are shocked by her behaviour and complete lack of shame. She behaves as if nothing out of the ordinary has happened, and tells them how she has been showing off her wedding ring from the window of their carriage. Wickham's behaviour is equally impudent: he resumes his old charming manners

without a hint that he is in any way to blame. Elizabeth leaves the room
in disgust. At dinner Lydia dominates the conversation. She invites her
sisters to Newcastle for the winter and offers to 'get' them husbands.
Elizabeth coldly declines the suggestion.

Wickham and Lydia are to stay for ten days. One morning Lydia
insists on telling Elizabeth about her wedding. In her rambling narrative
she lets drop the fact that Darcy accompanied Wickham to the church.
In mentioning this, Lydia is breaking the promise of secrecy that both
men had sought with regard to Darcy's presence, so Elizabeth cannot ask
for further information. Once more she has to leave the room, but this
time because she cannot contain her curiosity. She writes a short letter to
her aunt, asking about the matter.

> The appearance of Lydia and Wickham in the family circle is
> depicted dramatically, and without authorial comment. Jane and
> Elizabeth's amazement at their impudence is comment enough.
> Mrs Bennet is all thoughtless pleasure at seeing her favourite
> daughter again; Mr Bennet is coldly and quietly angry; Elizabeth
> for once is so lost for words that she rushes out of the room. Later
> she finds her tongue when she sharply rebukes Lydia's offer to find
> her a husband.

> **Ironically** it is Lydia's incapacity to keep a solemnly sworn secret
> that puts Elizabeth into a fever of curiosity about Darcy. An
> instance of Lydia's empty-headed folly advances the **plot** so as to
> serve Elizabeth's interests. Jane is too honourable to press for
> further discussion of the matter, but Elizabeth cannot stop herself
> from writing to her aunt.

CHAPTER 52    Mrs Gardiner's long letter describes Darcy's role in
              bringing about Lydia's wedding. Elizabeth regrets
              the impossibility of ever marrying Darcy. She
              encounters Wickham

Mrs Gardiner replies immediately. She writes that she and her husband
had believed that Elizabeth was fully aware of Darcy's intervention.
Darcy was responsible for finding Wickham and Lydia. He reasoned
with them. Lydia would not leave Wickham, despite their not being

married. Wickham was not interested in marrying Lydia and still hoped to make his fortune in another match. Darcy bargained with Wickham and ended up paying his debts, totalling about a £1,000, buying his new commission in the army and settling an extra £1,000 on Lydia. He insisted that Mr Gardiner take the credit for the affair. Mrs Gardiner, in her letter, makes many allusions to another motive that Darcy may have had and praises Darcy's 'understanding and opinions'. She makes a teasing reference to visiting Elizabeth at Pemberley in the future.

After reading this letter Elizabeth is overcome by a storm of thoughts. She is fully aware of the enormous obligation that she and her family now bear Darcy. She regrets ever having treated him badly and is proud of the nobility of his behaviour.

Wickham appears. He asks her about her visit to Pemberley. Elizabeth shows that she knows more about his behaviour than he thinks. She reminds him that the church living was only promised him conditionally in the late Darcy's will, and that he had accepted money when he decided not to enter the church. She hints also that she knows of his actions with regard to Georgiana Darcy. She does not want to quarrel with him, and so reminds him that they are brother and sister thanks to his marriage with Lydia. He kisses her hand.

The reader sides with Mrs Gardiner rather than Elizabeth in her interpretation of Darcy's behaviour. Our sense of the comic texture and structure of the novel makes it reassuringly likely that Darcy's doings are prompted by his continued interest in Elizabeth. She cannot believe this is the case: it is impossible for her to imagine that Darcy would be prepared to be the brother-in-law of Wickham.

Elizabeth's verbal fencing with Wickham is an interesting example of how strong and intelligent she is, and how necessary in Austen's world it is to use language to take control of a situation. She makes clear by hints and allusions that she knows all there is to know about Wickham's wrongdoing in the past. She takes some pleasure in leaving him suitably embarrassed, while at the same time retaining that surface of politeness suitable to a sister-in-law.

CHAPTER 53    **Lydia and Wickham leave Longbourn for Newcastle. Bingley comes to Netherfield. He and Darcy visit Longbourn**

Lydia leaves Longbourn and will not return for at least a year. Mrs Bennet is disconsolate until she hears that Bingley is to return to Netherfield. Mrs Bennet asks her husband to visit Bingley, a repetition of her request with which the events of the novel began. Mr Bennet refuses, and Mrs Bennet is consoled by the decision to invite Bingley to dinner. Jane is much distressed to have to hear so much talk of him.

On the third morning after his arrival at Netherfield, accompanied by Darcy, Bingley is spotted riding towards Longbourn. Elizabeth reflects on how she is the only one that knows of Darcy's beneficial intervention in Lydia's marriage. Nobody knows that her feelings towards him have changed. She is astonished that he should come to see her, and determined not to assume too much about what this may mean. The guests arrive. Elizabeth is embarrassed by the exaggerated civility that Mrs Bennet shows towards Bingley, and her coldness to Darcy. Darcy is silent and less friendly than he was when they met at Pemberley. Mrs Bennet boasts of Lydia's marriage and makes a pointed reference to Darcy's supposed treatment of Mr Wickham. Jane's beauty seems to be affecting Bingley. As they leave Mrs Bennet invites her guests to dinner.

Austen is preoccupied in this chapter with Elizabeth's reactions to the development of seeing Darcy again, now that her feelings towards him have changed. We are shown events almost entirely from Elizabeth's point of view. Both Jane and Elizabeth guard themselves against inappropriate and immodest hopes with regard to Bingley and Darcy. In this they are contrasted with their mother, who is as unashamed as ever in her matchmaking, though **ironically** she is determined on being rude to Darcy. Her ignorance of the fact that Darcy has saved Lydia from 'irremediable infamy' and of Elizabeth's new-found partiality leads to much embarrassment. The reader can afford to view this as comic, since we have less to lose than Elizabeth in presuming to be sure that Darcy is intent on renewing his proposal.

CHAPTER 54    **Bingley and Darcy come to dinner**

Elizabeth goes for a walk to contemplate Darcy's behaviour. She is annoyed by his silence and wonders why he paid the visit. Jane joins her and insists that she and Bingley are merely 'indifferent acquaintances'.

Bingley and Darcy come to dinner, and Bingley chooses to sit next to Jane. Elizabeth sees him looking at Darcy as if asking permission. Darcy is next to Mrs Bennet and far from Elizabeth. She notes how little they speak and how coldly Mrs Bennet treats him. She hopes that she will be able to speak to Darcy during the course of the evening but finds herself too embroiled in serving coffee to exchange more than a few words with him.

The guests leave and Mrs Bennet comments on the success of the evening. The food was appreciated and she is sure that Bingley admires Jane. Jane continues to insist to Elizabeth that she feels nothing special for Bingley, and Elizabeth gently teases her.

The comedy of both sisters determined not to acknowledge their true feelings continues. Elizabeth can afford to hope the best for Jane, while trying to conceal the force of her own desires even from herself. Her irritation with Darcy's reserve is amusing to the reader, who sees it as consonant with his behaviour throughout the novel.

CHAPTER 55    **Bingley proposes to Jane and is accepted**

A few days later Bingley calls at Longbourn alone. Darcy has left for London and will return in ten days' time. He accepts an invitation for lunch the following day and arrives before the ladies are ready. Mrs Bennet rushes around in nervous anticipation. Jane refuses to go downstairs without one of her sisters. After tea, Mrs Bennet continues to contrive to leave Jane and Bingley alone together. She calls Elizabeth and Kitty from the room. Elizabeth does not argue with her, but soon returns to Jane's side. Bingley stays for supper and agrees to go shooting with Mr Bennet the following day. Now Jane does not say anything about being indifferent to Bingley. Elizabeth has every hope that her sister and Bingley may complete their relationship.

Bingley and Mr Bennet go shooting as planned. Mr Bennet finds Bingley pleasant company and he is invited to dinner that evening.

Elizabeth retires to write a letter, and, on returning to the drawing room, surprises Jane and Bingley in private conversation. Bingley leaves the room and Jane confesses that she is 'the happiest creature in the world'. Bingley has gone to ask Mr Bennet's permission to marry Jane. Jane is overjoyed and goes to tell her mother the good news. Bingley returns and Elizabeth congratulates him. Jane tells Elizabeth that Bingley did not know that she was in London during the spring. She blames it on his sisters.

Jane's happiness is shown to be true and deserved, and her expressions of delight can be compared to the hollowness of Mr Collins's much-repeated phrase 'happiest of men' earlier in the novel. Austen does not attempt to show how Jane and Bingley talk to each other, preferring the safety of seeing events from Elizabeth's point of view. Similarly we are not provided with Elizabeth's congratulatory speech to Jane. Much of the plan of these final chapters, in which Elizabeth is still in suspense as to Darcy's intentions, is to temper the possible sentimentality of the happy ending for which we are still confidently hoping. Austen wants to show how proper, intelligent, demure young women should behave.

At the end of this chapter, the fickleness of public opinion and sentiment is mocked by Austen: 'The Bennets were speedily pronounced to be the luckiest family in the world, though only a few weeks before ... they had been generally proved to be marked out for misfortune'. The semi-legal verbs 'pronounced' and 'proved' **ironically** draw attention to the worthlessness and insubstantiality of public opinion, though at least here the neighbours are taking pleasure in the Bennets' good fortune, rather than, as before, delighting in their downfall.

CHAPTER 56    **Lady Catherine pays a surprise visit. She attempts to extort a promise from Elizabeth that she will never accept Darcy. Elizabeth refuses to comply**

A week after Bingley and Jane have been engaged, a carriage arrives. Much to everyone's surprise it is Lady Catherine de Bourgh. She comments adversely on the small size of the Bennet's grounds and the inconvenience of their sitting room before asking Elizabeth to go for a walk with her. Lady Catherine launches into her subject. She has heard that Elizabeth may marry her nephew and asks Elizabeth to confirm the rumour as a 'scandalous falsehood'. Elizabeth is astonished by her address and does not answer her directly. Lady Catherine tells her that Darcy and Miss De Bourgh were destined for each other from infancy, and reminds Elizabeth that she is inferior in birth, connections and fortune. In the end Elizabeth admits that she is not engaged to Darcy, but refuses to promise that she would never accept him. Lady Catherine leaves, and is 'most seriously displeased'. Elizabeth does not answer her and returns indoors. Mrs Bennet assumes that Lady Catherine has called to bring some news of Charlotte. Elizabeth does not correct her, and even has to lie to conceal the true nature of the argument.

Though Jane Austen is shy of presenting lovers dramatically, she has no such timidity when presenting Lady Catherine's outraged and insulting snobbery in full flood. Elizabeth's confident rebuttal of all Lady Catherine's insults and demands is almost thrilling. Here is pride and prejudice in all its irrational fury, and it fails to prevail against a young woman's good sense. **Ironically** Lady Catherine's efforts speed the union of Darcy and Elizabeth, exactly the opposite of her intention (see Chapter 58).

CHAPTER 57    **Mr Collins writes to convey Lady Catherine's views. Mr Bennet shares his amusement at the letter with Elizabeth**

Elizabeth wonders about Lady Catherine's visit. How would Darcy respond to such an attack? She imagines that he will never come to see her again.

The next day Mr Bennet calls Elizabeth to his library. Mr Collins has written to him about her connection with Darcy. Mr Bennet, unaware of Elizabeth's sentiments towards Darcy, finds the letter ridiculous – particularly since it names Darcy as Elizabeth's suitor. Mr Collins conveys Lady Catherine's opposition to the match. He also expresses his shock that Lydia and Wickham have been allowed to visit Longbourn.

Elizabeth is forced to laugh at her father's jokes, when she would rather cry. The necessity of Elizabeth concealing her feelings is depicted as painful for her, but such misunderstandings are typical of comic situations, and the reader is still sure that the book in hand is indeed a comedy.

The scene serves also to point out Mr Bennet's lack of insight and show how his ironic vision insulates him from a sympathetic and lively interest in those around him. Lizzy is his favourite daughter, and yet he has not noticed anything about her state of feelings. The capacity to penetrate the surface of events, and understand the realities of proper feeling and morality behind it, is a highly prized attribute in Jane Austen's created world. Of course the narrator has more 'penetration' that any of the characters, since she knows how things are going to end.

CHAPTER 58    **Elizabeth finds herself alone with Darcy. She explains that her feelings have changed towards him. They discuss their relationship**

A few days after Lady Catherine's visit, Bingley brings Darcy to Longbourn. Kitty, Jane, Elizabeth, Bingley and Darcy go for a walk, and Kitty stops off at Lucas Lodge to visit Maria Lucas. Elizabeth, now alone with Darcy, is determined to discuss how matters stand between them. She tells him that she knows how he helped Wickham and Lydia and thanks him for his intervention. Darcy is embarrassed, and, in reply to her thanks, explains that he acted for her alone. In response to his direct question, Elizabeth is able to tell him that her feelings have changed since April. Darcy's renewed proposal is accepted by Elizabeth, with great happiness to them both. They walk and talk.

Elizabeth discovers that she has Lady Catherine to thank for his visit. Lady Catherine had told him of Elizabeth's refusal to promise not to accept him. Darcy realised that Elizabeth might care for him. They go over all that has happened between them in the past. He tells Elizabeth that she was right to refuse him at his first proposal. He has memorised her reproofs to him and admits to having behaved terribly. Darcy acknowledges that he was spoiled as a child and almost encouraged to be 'selfish and overbearing'. Elizabeth mentions his altered behaviour at

Pemberley and he tells her that his aim was to convince her that he was sufficiently generous to forget the past. Elizabeth discovers that before Darcy left for London he told Bingley that Jane was not indifferent to him. He had observed her behaviour and was convinced that Elizabeth was right about her sister's feelings. Bingley was angry when he found out that his friend had prevented him from seeing Jane while she was in London, but his anger soon passed when Jane returned his affections.

It is Elizabeth who initiates the serious and intimate conversation that occupies this chapter. Both of them have to explain the true state of their feelings with regard to each other at every stage in the haphazard development of their relationship. They both have a lot to make up for, since this is the first time they have talked alone since the awful scene of his refused proposal. The necessity for explanation, confession and apology is fulfilled. Most noticeable is the way in which Elizabeth instigates the conversation, and shows her control at the end, by holding back from teasing Darcy.

Before the deserved 'happiness' can be fully allowed, they must map out the rights and wrongs of how they have behaved and arrive at a true understanding of what was and was not appropriate. It was her reproof of Darcy's failure to behave in a 'more gentleman-like manner' that stung him into rethinking his mode of behaviour. Manners here stand not merely for polish, but for the essence of the way sensitive and intelligent human beings should behave towards each other.

At the moment when Elizabeth and Darcy are most involved in confessing their love for each other, the narrator shies away from putting into words what passes between them. Is Austen incapable of imagining this crucial passage of feeling when Darcy renews his proposal? Or is there merely a special propriety in leaving such a moment to the imaginations of her readers, so as to avoid the bathetic joining of highly charged feelings with banal and clichéed phrases?

CHAPTER 59    **Elizabeth confesses all to an astonished Jane. The next day Mr Bennet gives his consent, and Mrs Bennet has to revise her opinion of Darcy**

Elizabeth and Darcy are late home. They eat dinner and spend the evening in each other's company. That night Elizabeth confesses her engagement to Jane. To begin with, Jane can only think Elizabeth is joking. She cannot believe that Elizabeth loves Darcy, and is worried that they will not be happy together. Elizabeth explains jokingly that she first fell in love with Darcy when she saw Pemberley, but then she gives Jane a solemn promise of her attachment. Jane is happy for her but reproaches her for keeping so many secrets. Elizabeth explains the complicated motives for her silence, and tells Jane about Darcy's role in Lydia's marriage.

The next day Mrs Bennet complains that the 'disagreeable Mr Darcy' is with 'our dear Bingley'. She asks Elizabeth if she will be so kind as to walk with Darcy, and allow Jane and Bingley to be together. The two couples go for a walk. Darcy resolves to ask Mr Bennet's permission that evening, and Elizabeth decides to ask her mother's. Darcy returns from Mr Bennet's library and sends Elizabeth to her father. He asks her if she is 'out of her senses' to accept Darcy and is worried that she is making a terrible mistake. Finally Elizabeth manages to convince him that Darcy is truly the man of her choice. Elizabeth joins her mother in her dressing room and tells her the news. Mrs Bennet is silent for a little while, while she absorbs this extraordinary news, but is soon delighted. She is overcome at the thought of what the couple's income and style of life will be.

Elizabeth is pleased to see that her father is making an effort to get to know Darcy, and luckily Mrs Bennet is a little more reserved in the presence of Darcy himself.

This is a chapter of high comedy, in which Elizabeth has to face the consequence of disguising her true feelings for so long. First Jane has to be convinced, then her father, then her mother. Each responds in their own way. Jane keeps wanting Elizabeth to be more serious. Mr Bennet is admirable in his real concern that Lizzy should only marry someone that she truly respects. We should see this as a comment on his own marriage, as well as a proper understanding of Elizabeth. He is less admirable in his complacent pleasure in the fact that he will not have to pay Darcy back for the saving of Lydia and Wickham.

Mrs Bennet is quickly won over by a moment's thought about Darcy's wealth. She is soon dwelling on how rich Elizabeth will become, and how handsome and charming the 'disagreeable Darcy' has suddenly turned out to be. Finally she wishes to know what is Darcy's favourite food: money, appearances and food preoccupy her, all relative trivialities for Elizabeth and Austen.

CHAPTER 60 **Letters are exchanged. Elizabeth looks forward to being at Pemberley**

Elizabeth questions Darcy about how and when he fell in love with her. She asks him whether he admired her for her 'impertinence'. The two lovers quibble happily about their past behaviour. Elizabeth is playful, Darcy is more formal. Darcy writes to Lady Catherine about their engagement while Elizabeth writes her long overdue reply to Mrs Gardiner, inviting her to Pemberley for Christmas. Mr Bennet writes a curt letter to Mr Collins to advise him of Elizabeth's impending marriage: he should placate Lady Catherine, 'but if I were you, I would stand by the nephew. He has more to give'. Miss Bingley writes to Jane to congratulate her. Miss Darcy is overjoyed to hear of her brother's engagement. The Collins arrive at Lucas Lodge, anxious to avoid the storm of Lady Catherine's displeasure. Elizabeth is pleased to see Darcy tolerating Mr Collins and Sir William Lucas. Luckily Mrs Philips and Mrs Bennet, awed by his presence, are less offensive in Darcy's company than they are with the more open Bingley, but Elizabeth tries to keep Darcy to herself.

Elizabeth is playful in trying to establish exactly when Darcy fell in love with her, but there is a psychological truth in her explanation, from which Darcy does not refuse to concur. So accustomed is he to have women like Miss Bingley fawning on him that her freedom of spirit in teasing him made her especially attractive. It is indeed her 'impudence' that has made her attractive, rather than repelling him.

Austen provides the text of Elizabeth's letter to her aunt. It is full of **ironic** exaggerations. We are not shown what Darcy writes to Lady Catherine. Mr Bennet's letter to Mr Collins is wholly lacking in the ironic politeness that is usually his mode of dealing with the pompous clergyman. In recommending Mr Collins to court Darcy rather than his aunt, it cuts right through the hypocrisy of Mr Collins's need to court favour with the powerful in order to secure suitably profitable advancement in the church.

If dealing honestly with money is an occasionally surprising but consistent aspect of the narrative, Austen is equally unsentimental in portraying the difficulties that confront Elizabeth with regard to her relatives' lack of good manners and sophistication. Darcy must be prevented whenever possible from having to deal with Mrs Bennet and Mrs Philips. In *Pride and Prejudice* as in Austen's other novels, the witty and good illustrate by their forbearance and courtesy the proper way of dealing with bores and the tasteless. Darcy's duty is to be unfailingly polite. However, in the next chapter we see that even someone so unfailingly good-natured as Bingley moves away from the neighbourhood of his in-laws as soon as is decently possible.

CHAPTER 61    Resumé

Some time has passed. Both Jane and Elizabeth are happily married. Mrs Bennet is happy but no less silly than ever. Mr Bennet misses Elizabeth and often pays surprise visits to Pemberley. After a year at Netherfield the Bingleys move to within thirty miles of Pemberley. Kitty improves thanks to the time that she spends with her older sisters. Mary stays at home to work on her 'accomplishments' and to keep her mother company. Lydia and Wickham live an 'unsettled' life, overspending their income and moving continually. Elizabeth often sends Lydia money that she has saved from her own expenses. Lydia is even allowed to visit Pemberley when Darcy is away. Miss Bingley, 'mortified' by Darcy's marriage, manages to arrive at dealing politely with Elizabeth so as to retain the right of visiting at Pemberley. Georgiana Darcy and Elizabeth are very close, although Georgiana is often alarmed by Elizabeth's 'lively, sportive' way of treating Darcy. Lady Catherine writes an abusive letter to Darcy, but eventually is prevailed upon to forgive the couple, and even visits Pemberley, propelled chiefly by her curiosity to see how Elizabeth is coping. Elizabeth and Darcy remain on very close terms with the Gardiners whom they deem responsible for having brought them together.

In this final chapter the narrator closes up all the loose ends of the narrative with a 'happily ever after' explanation of all that awaits the characters. Any easy fairytale sentiment is kept well at bay by the clipped, detached and **ironic** mode of description in which she sums up events.

Mr Bennet delighted in going to Pemberley, 'especially when he was least expected'. Mary, it is suggested, relaxes into moralising 'over every morning visit', once her two more attractive sisters are no longer rivals. We are shown Lydia's letter to Elizabeth: it is astonishingly crude and bold in its egocentric application for help and money.

The reader is pleased to hear that Elizabeth's spirit is in no way dampened by marriage. Georgiana is wide-eyed at Elizabeth's bold manner of speaking to Darcy.

The final sentence refers to the Darcy's affection for the Gardiners, and their gratitude towards them for bringing Elizabeth to Derbyshire so as to be 'the means of uniting them'.

# PART THREE

# CRITICAL APPROACHES

## CHARACTERISATION

Through the ironic narrator, Jane Austen seems to enjoy discussing her characters, recounting their conversations with each other, and showing how they behave both in times of leisure and of stress. For further discussion of the narrator see Narrative Techniques. However, self-sufficient though they may seem, the characters are only part of the novelist's plan to discuss a number of ideas through the narration of a series of events. When writing as a literary critic it is necessary to keep a sharp sense of their fictive nature in relation to discovering what this overall plan might be.

One striking aspect of Austen's writing is that she is surprisingly non-descriptive. We are rarely told much about what the characters look like in any specific way. Where she does indulge in more specific and individuating comment, it is usually in direct connection with that character's place in the action or the moral framework of the story. For example, we are told in Chapter 2 that Lydia, though the youngest, is the tallest of the five sisters. These comments must be seen in relation to her behaviour: at sixteen she is physically a woman, but emotionally immature and out of control. Austen has little interest in inventing an appearance for her characters. Darcy is captivated by 'a pair of fine eyes in the face of a pretty woman'. When 'with great intrepidity' he admits these are Elizabeth's (Chapter 6), his comment is remorselessly used against him by Miss Bingley (who had expected a compliment to herself). Elizabeth's beautiful eyes – we are told they are 'dark' – therefore serve a larger purpose than simple description. They allow Darcy to stand up for her and for himself, and then they serve Caroline Bingley with an opportunity for malice.

What finally interests the narrator is not her characters' appearance, but their moral qualities, or lack of them. Through their attitudes to these their differences are revealed, and they show their discrimination and capacity for good taste and judgement.

## Elizabeth Bennet

Elizabeth is the second oldest of the Bennet sisters, and is used by the narrator more than any other character in the novel as a **centre of consciousness** from which to view events. In the sense that she is the main focus of the reader's interest, she is the novel's heroine, though she makes mistakes, and is not particularly heroic. In the novel's concern with pride and with prejudice, she and Darcy are the main players. She is Mr Bennet's favourite daughter, intelligent and lively, and her 'quickness' of mind is made evident in her taste for witty and teasing conversation, where she likes to adopt striking and independent views. Evidence for this is best found in Chapters 8, 9 and 11, when she is looking after Jane at Netherfield, in her conversations with Bingley, his sisters and Darcy.

She likes to laugh at people, including herself. We are told after Darcy refused to dance with her, that 'she told the story with great spirit amongst her friends; for she had a lively, playful disposition, which delighted in anything ridiculous' (Chapter 3). It is this quality of humour that attracts Darcy. Her rival Miss Bingley calls it 'that little something, bordering on conceit and impertinence' (Chapter 10), but the narrator has already told us that 'there was a mixture of sweetness and archness in her manner which made it difficult for her to affront anybody'. She shares her capacity for **irony** with her father, and with the narrator. This allows her to stand away from situations and offer judgements on them, sometimes (though not as often as the narrator or her father), in the form of saying the opposite of what she really means. 'Mr Darcy is all politeness' she remarks in Chapter 6, as a way of avoiding dancing with him: we can guess she is remembering his rudeness to her.

She is active and robust, to the point of being indecorous and unfeminine, from the point of view of her enemies. 'Elizabeth continued her walk alone ... springing over puddles with impatient activity, and finding herself at last within view of the house, with weary ancles, dirty stockings, and a face glowing with the warmth of exercise' (Chapter 7). Her dirty petticoat is shocking to Miss Bingley. However, Darcy and Bingley find the results of her vigour attractive.

As the book progresses we start to share more of Elizabeth's thoughts, and see her more inwardly, often by means of the technique called **free indirect discourse** or thought, where we are presented thoughts in the manner of indirect speech. A key passage in reviewing Elizabeth's growth is Chapter 36, when we see her painfully coming to terms with her mistaken understanding of Wickham and Darcy while reading Darcy's letter. She has to take in information which contradicts some of her prejudiced judgements, and in doing so realises that she has not been as sharp a reader of character as she has confidently supposed. She blames herself for not having recognised the smack of 'impropriety' in Wickham's behaviour, but allowed herself to be deceived by his charm.

Another less grievous misunderstanding is her astonishment at Charlotte Lucas's acceptance of Mr Collins as a husband. This follows naturally enough from their earlier discussion as to whether happiness in marriage depends upon prior mutual knowledge or merely chance (Chapter 6). Elizabeth feels with some indignation that Charlotte has sacrificed 'every better feeling to worldly advantage' (end of Chapter 22). And yet Charlotte, who was not 'romantic', was twenty-seven years old, and was 'so *very* plain' seems happy enough with her idiotic husband when Elizabeth stays with her in Kent.

'Worldly advantage' is what Elizabeth gains in her marriage too. How much is she joking when she remarks that she fell in love with Darcy when she saw Pemberley? Is one of the lessons that Elizabeth has to learn, to place true value on Darcy's wealth and position, the very source of his pride? In relation to her early conversation with Charlotte, Elizabeth has stuck by her opinion that bride and groom should know some of each other's faults, and merits, before marriage. But the reader is left to wonder what part the unromantic financial aspect has in helping provide a foundation for the turnabout in Elizabeth's feelings.

Only Darcy and Elizabeth develop as characters in *Pride and Prejudice*. Perhaps it is a matter of their superior intelligence that they are marked out by the narrator as capable of moral evolution in a way that their friends, neighbours and relatives are not. Or it may just be an aspect of novelistic convention to concentrate only on the 'juvenile leads' as they would be called in the theatre, the paired young **protagonist** and **antagonist** around whom the story revolves.

## JANE BENNET

Jane is the eldest, the most sweet tempered and by general agreement the most beautiful of the Bennet sisters. We have no idea about her appearance except that she is heavier than Elizabeth and cannot run as fast as her (Chapter 49). Bingley, after two dances with her at the first assembly, says that she is the 'most beautiful creature I have beheld' (Chapter 3). She is optimistic, patient and constant in her affections, as her long wait for Bingley shows. Jane is candid, in the old meaning of the word: she looks at the world without bias or malice. Candour is the opposite of prejudice. The two sisters' reactions to Lydia's elopement is typical: Mrs Gardiner, also optimistic, remarks: 'Jane ... does not think so ill of Wickham as to believe him capable of the attempt' (Chapter 47). Jane's essential, almost stereotypical goodness makes her a perfect foil for the more difficult Elizabeth, and a means by which the development of Elizabeth's character change can be mapped.

## LYDIA BENNET

Lydia is fully developed physically at fifteen: 'she had high animal spirits, and a sort of natural self-consequence, which the attentions of the officers, to whom her uncle's good dinners and her own easy manners recommended her, had increased into assurance' (Chapter 9). 'Animal', 'easy', and 'assurance' are all danger signals in one so young. Does 'animal' hint at her sexuality? She is her mother's favourite daughter, and shares with her a partiality for men in uniform and an obsession with fashionable clothes. She is brazenly flirtatious, hungry for the admiration of any man, and vain. In the world of Austen's novels irresponsibility over small things, like lunch money (see Chapter 39) can presage future disasters on a larger scale. Lydia lacks all understanding – or does not care – about the moral and social consequences of running away with Wickham. Her unworried expectation that living with him would probably lead to marriage at some time or other, is profoundly shocking to Jane and Elizabeth, and even their father.

In our time we do not all regard premarital sex as a moral crime, and we might choose to see something positive in Lydia's 'assurance', some modern 'girl power' certainly lacking in, say, Jane. The novel allows us to see Lydia clearly enough from her sisters' perspective – she is thoughtless, superficial, selfish, egocentric. Marriage for Lydia is no more than an opportunity for 'very good fun' (Chapter 51). Her disappearance causes a family furore, but **ironically** it is the means by which Darcy and Elizabeth will be reconciled. Darcy's innocent sister Georgiana was also prey to Wickham's charms, allowing Darcy to sympathise with the Bennet predicament, and even to feel himself somewhat to blame.

## MARY AND CATHERINE BENNET

Mary is the middle sister, and the family's pedant, taking refuge in books like her father, but she has not learnt ironic detachment in them. She is self-important, pious, moralistic and boring. Mary plays the piano mechanically well, but without feeling, and for much longer than anyone wants to listen. At the end of Chapter 5 she delivers a dreary little monologue on pride. As it deals with one of the book's explicit **themes**, it is not without interest as a textbook statement of the difference between pride and vanity, and shows that Austen can use Mary as a mouthpiece for a point-of-view, concealing a serious distinction in comic pomposity. However, she is generally ignored, though her father sometimes enjoys teasing her. At the end of the story, the narrator hints at tensions that lie behind her role in the family: 'Mary was obliged to mix more with the world ... and as she was no longer mortified by comparisons between her sisters' beauty and her own, it was suspected by her father that she submitted to the change without much reluctance' (Chapter 61). This is the only example of her development as a character, and indeed so constant is her minor role in the **plot** that she is something of a **caricature**.

Catherine or Kitty, second youngest sister, also plays little part in the novel except as a parallel and contrast to Lydia, with whom she is connected in the enthusiastic pursuit of officers till Lydia's removal to Brighton. She is being led astray by Lydia, till the better influences of her older sisters take over, so successfully, we are informed in the conclusion that she becomes 'less ignorant, less irritable and less insipid' (Chapter 61).

# Mr BENNET

Mr Bennet is clever in his **ironic** mockery of his wife and daughters, but ultimately morally indolent and self-indulgent. The reader finds him funnier than his family does. He represents the dangers of an ironic disposition unmixed with the starch of energetic moral and social probity, a virtue possessed by his fellow ironists, Elizabeth and the narrator. His failure to follow Elizabeth's advice not to allow Lydia to go to Brighton (Chapter 41) is the clearest example of his misjudgement; at least he has the grace to admit this and apologise (Chapter 48). Though he fails to live up to his responsibilities as father and head of the family, he remains the source of pleasant jokes right up to the end of the book: 'I admire all my three sons-in-law highly ... Wickham, perhaps, is my favourite' (Chapter 60).

Several factors are shown as having forged his personality. The entail of Longbourn hangs over him, but he has put off doing anything about it, hoping still for the birth of a son that would put things to rights (Chapter 50). So his family is in a state of insecurity: Mrs Bennet is right to worry about this, though her fretting does nothing to help the situation. His casual acceptance of the financial resolution of Lydia's marriage shows how inactive he can be. Mr Bennet's pleasure at not having to do anything seems too easy and superficial a response. We cannot admire his indolence, his fecklessness or his uselessness in the face of the grave situation in which the family finds itself. Mr Gardiner and Darcy take over tracing and dealing with Wickham and Lydia. At this point in the novel his humour deserts him, but not for long (Chapter 48); but would he be more likeable if he sunk into depressive gloom? He at least has found a way of dealing cheerfully with an unhappy marriage and five daughters.

The gulf in understanding between him and his wife is huge. The narrator explains that he married for a love based on his wife's youth and beauty (Chapter 42). Their marriage represents a warning of such an irrational and impetuous approach to domestic happiness.

## Mrs bennet

Whereas we can laugh with Mr Bennet, we laugh at Mrs Bennet. Our view of her is pickled in the narrator's acidic summary very early in the text: 'she was a woman of mean understanding, little information, and uncertain temper. When she was discontented, she fancied herself nervous. The business of her life was getting her daughters married; its solace was visiting and news' (Chapter 1). It is her 'business' around which the novel revolves, and which instigates the **plot**. It is also her behaviour – her vulgarity – that is the main obstacle to Darcy's developing interest in Elizabeth and his reason for persuading Bingley to leave Meryton and ignore Jane.

It is not the position of the Bennet family, but their manners that shocks Darcy. He characterises their behaviour at the Netherfield ball in his letter to Elizabeth: 'the situation of your mother's family, though objectionable, was as nothing in comparison of that total want of propriety so frequently, so almost uniformly betrayed by herself, by your three younger sisters, and occasionally even by your father'. The language may be different but the situation is familiar: a young person is cruelly embarrassed by the behaviour of her parents in a public place.

Mrs Bennet's stupidity is on display during almost every crisis in the novel. She shows an incapacity to argue rationally rather than simply give way to her feelings, and this leads her to contradict herself in a comical rush of nonsensical attitudes. A good example of this is in Chapter 23, after Sir William Lucas has announced Charlotte's engagement. Her reaction demonstrates her inability to disguise or recognise her self-pity, malice, and naked rivalry with her neighbours, and her inability to think rationally. Later on, in her blind pleasure at Lydia's marriage with Wickham, she shows a more alarming blindness to financial and moral propriety.

Mrs Bennet is portrayed as superficial in her understanding, trivial in her interests and mistaken in her judgements throughout the whole novel. Mostly this is openly comical, but sometimes it is almost sad that she is so incapable of responding to situations with more good sense and less nagging complaint and hysterical silliness. In so far as **caricatures** present a view of unchangeable human character, their clowning often has this distressing aspect.

## M R BINGLEY

Bingley, the 'single man in possession of a good fortune' who sets the book going, is kind, easy-going, attracted by beautiful young women with whom he enjoys dancing, and, compared to his friend Darcy, somewhat unreflective. It is this difference between them that Darcy likes: the 'easiness, openness, ductility of his temper' (Chapter 4). Chapters 7 to 12 when Elizabeth stays at Netherfield Park are worth rereading with care in the light of what happens later in the novel, as they lay the foundation for many of the book's **themes**, such as the nature of character, friendship and pride.

The most striking example of Bingley's 'ductility' is the way he allows Darcy to persuade him to leave Netherfield. In the book's resolution he is equally ductile, falling easily back in love with Jane, now that he enjoys the approval of this friend. He is the perfect mate for Jane. They share the same sunny optimism with regard to human behaviour. Being less 'intricate' means that neither develop as characters, in contrast with the other pair at the centre of the book's interests, Elizabeth and Darcy.

## M R DARCY

Darcy is in many respects repulsive at the start of the novel. Austen seems to enjoy creating difficult characters, but Darcy is difficult to accept in a manner quite different from her **caricatures**. He is proud, and he is prejudiced – and in common with Elizabeth we dislike him for this – but we are asked to consider whether sometimes such feelings may be appropriate. We are told that 'Darcy was clever. He was at the same time haughty, reserved, and fastidious, and his manners, though well bred, were not inviting ... he was continually giving offence' (Chapter 4). As with Bingley, the conversations in Chapters 7 to 11 repay close attention in thinking about the establishment and future development of Darcy's character. In Chapter 11 Elizabeth manages to confront him with some of his potential failings, in witty discussion of the fact that 'Mr Darcy is not to be laughed at'. She concludes that he is implacably resentful and hates everybody. (See Textual Analysis: Text 1.)

The larger events of the novel show that Darcy is not at all implacably resentful. In his careful, dignified and secretive pursuit of

Elizabeth after her angry refusal of his proposal, Darcy is shown to be more capable of change than any other character in the novel, Elizabeth included. He is drawn to Bingley by the contrast in their personalities, and this seems to be also the attraction that Elizabeth presents – she can supply a cheerfulness and good nature that he knows himself to lack.

Another key passage in exploring Darcy's development is his pained, honest and self-critical letter to Elizabeth (Chapter 35). No other character is shown to be capable of such penetrating self-analysis.

Honesty and self-analysis notwithstanding, Darcy can and does give offence by his behaviour. At his first meeting with Meryton society, when he will dance only with Bingley's sisters, and when he generally disparages the company, he slights Elizabeth in her hearing in a manner parallel with Mrs Bennet's insult to him at the Netherfield Park ball. There may be an element of shyness in his reserve and haughty disdain, but that is perhaps a contemporary way of looking at such behaviour. The narrator does not portray Darcy as shy, and shyness is not part of the propriety of a gentleman, who should be equal to all the occasions in which he finds himself. Darcy is poor at dealing with other people, and with his own feelings, which come upon him as a surprise. His proposal to Elizabeth (Chapter 34) is wrong in strategy and very tactlessly expressed. Elizabeth's final insulting refusal is spoken with the exaggerations of rage, but it is not unfair (see Chapter 34).

As readers we have witnessed what truth there is in Elizabeth's view of Darcy's manners towards herself and her family; in so far as the narrator has often taken her side, we feel some pleasure in her outburst. She is wrongly angry at Darcy's treatment of Wickham, but rightly angry at his removal of Bingley from Jane's company. He was wrong about Jane's feelings, and in this he lacked penetration, that ability to see what lies behind situations. In his intricacy of character, poor, proud Darcy has much to learn before the novel can arrive at the satisfactory conclusion of his marriage to Elizabeth.

## WICKHAM

George Wickham's behaviour includes seducing young girls, financial deals that are not far from blackmail and extortion, and running away from debts. Above all he is a danger to the impressionable young women of Jane Austen's social world. Does his name suggest 'wicked'? He is not a paedophile: the narrator makes it clear that Georgiana Darcy, the first of his victims of whom we are told, is physically mature: 'though little more than sixteen, her figure was formed' (Chapter 44). His dangerousness lies in the fact that he combines a handsome appearance and charming manners with an absolute lack of veracity and sexual morality, 'vicious propensities' to which Darcy alludes in his letter (Chapter 35), that are almost unbelievable in the drawing rooms of Hertfordshire.

When first sighted in Meryton, he caught 'the attention of every young lady'; his appearance was greatly in his favour; he also had 'a happy readiness of conversation'(Chapter 15). Elizabeth, who believes a young man ought to be handsome 'if he possibly can' (Chapter 4), is instantly attracted to him, and he to her: 'Mr Wickham was the happy man towards whom almost every female eye was turned, and Elizabeth was the happy woman by whom he finally seated himself' (Chapter 16). Darcy set off something of a similar stir at the first public assembly, but that was caused by the rumour of his wealth, and of course he and Wickham are in many respects absolute opposites. While Wickham seduces young women outside the public eye, to the great distress of their families, Darcy is dedicated to concealing his good deeds, as in the rescue of Lydia. Several times Elizabeth argues that Wickham's good looks prove his honesty – a very foolish line of argument.

Chapter 16, in which Wickham falsely recounts his relationship with Darcy, repays close rereading in comparison with Darcy's true version of the same events in his letter (Chapter 35). Much of what Wickham says is accurate. But the gloss he puts on events is entirely false, and he omits to say anything about the money that Darcy provided and he wasted. Of course he says nothing of his plan to elope with Georgiana Darcy. With all the skills of a confidence trickster he is very careful not to tell any direct lies that will be easily detected. Elizabeth leads Wickham on to incriminate the 'abominable' Darcy. Prejudice blinds her. Jane wisely remarks that they do not know enough about either man to be sure what is the truth of the matter, but Elizabeth ascribes this simply to Jane's sunny disposition (Chapter 17). Caroline Bingley, whom Elizabeth heartily dislikes ('insolent girl!'), warns her quite accurately against Wickham, but she puts this down to jealousy and spite (Chapter 18).

From Mrs Gardiner's letter to Elizabeth, in which she explains Darcy's role in the bringing about the marriage of the runaways, we learn what Wickham's motives were (Chapter 52). Marriage 'had never been *his* design'. His gambling debts forced him to leave his regiment, and he took Lydia with him for company, blaming her insistence, with no heed to the consequences of such a 'disgraceful situation' for Lydia and her family. He has no plan for the future, except to marry money – and Lydia does not have enough of this to make her an interesting partner. The narrator does not spell the matter out, but we must assume that Wickham's interest in Lydia is sexual – she is otherwise of no use to him. Lydia is portrayed as wholly infatuated: 'she was sure that they would be married some time or other, and it did not much signify when'.

When Wickham meets Elizabeth as his sister-in-law, we are shown how he sets about still to charm her, in the hopes that she still does not know the full extent of his infamy. She makes it clear by a few hints that he can no longer deceive her. He shows some embarrassment – he bites his lips, and 'hardly knew how to look' (Chapter 52), but remorse or guilt are not in his vocabulary of behaviour. Wickham is not a character that changes, but he is one of whom we learn much more as the narrative progresses. His part in the **plot** demonstrates the differences that can exist between appearance and reality, for the edification of the reader.

## MR COLLINS

Mr Collins's character is clear and consistent even from before his very first appearance in the novel. His first letter to Mr Bennet reveals him wholly. 'There is something very pompous in his stile ... Can he be a sensible man, sir?' Elizabeth asks her father. 'No my dear; I think not. I have great hopes of finding him quite the reverse. There is a mixture of servility and self-importance in his letter which promises well' (Chapter 13). At every point Mr Collins lives up to Mr Bennet's **ironic** hopes. His incessant harping on his attachments to Lady Catherine and Rosings, his irritating catch-phrases – 'the happiest of men', 'humble abode' – the utter predictability and triviality of his views, every aspect of his speech brands him as a monster of foolish self-congratulation. So much is he a

**caricature** that he is almost in danger of boring the reader. The narrator seems impatient with her own creation when, as often happens, she sums up his repetitive conversations via reported speech.

Novels are too frivolous for Mr Collins to read to the Bennet family (Chapter 14). We are reading a novel, so we are likely to disagree with this opinion. Yet he sees backgammon, losing money at whist, and dancing at balls as perfectly dignified activities. In his intentions of marriage he changes from Jane to Elizabeth 'while Mrs Bennet was poking the fire' (Chapter 15), and so his proposing to Charlotte three days after Elizabeth has turned him down is scarcely surprising to the reader. Nevertheless it shows an absolute lack of any of the proper feelings that ought to accompany a proposal of marriage.

Mr Collins reveals a cruelly unsympathetic aspect to his character in his letter to the Bennets concerning Lydia's elopement: 'The death of your daughter would have been a blessing in comparison of this … Let me advise you … to throw off your unworthy child from your affection for ever, and to leave her to reap the fruits of her own heinous offence' (Chapter 48). Later he recommends that 'you certainly ought to forgive them as christians, but never to admit them in your sight.' 'That is his notion of christian forgiveness!' comments Mr Bennet (Chapter 57).

Though Wickham might have become a clergyman, Mr Collins is the only representative of the Church in *Pride and Prejudice*. He offers several pronouncements on his duties during the novel, but they all revolve around his own self-aggrandising pride and conceit.

## LADY CATHERINE DE BOURGH

Like Mr Collins, his patroness Lady Catherine is a fixed character of exaggerated propensities, a caricature, in her case representing the extremes of snobbish pride and prejudice, which he is only too happy to absorb and reflect. Learning about her from Mr Collins prepares us for the worst, and when we see her in action at Rosings she fulfils our every expectation. She is high-handed, interfering, rude, overbearing, and infatuated with her position and the justice of her own opinions, many of which are plainly absurd. Her claims to excellence in music for example, are based on nothing but the presumption of her own authority: she does not play, yet she offers advice on practice and technique to one and all. When she rudely suggests Elizabeth would not be in the way if she practised on the second-best piano in Rosings, Darcy 'looked a little ashamed of his aunt's ill-breeding'. However distinguished her family may be, Austen shows us that her manners are appalling. Her ladyship represents an aristocratic parallel to Mrs Bennet.

The logic of Lady Catherine's behaviour is also wanting. Her visit to Longbourn (Chapter 56) to dissuade Elizabeth from accepting Darcy reaches a point almost of farce in its blustering foolishness. In her encounter with Elizabeth she fails to carry her purpose, and the reader delights in Elizabeth's rational and forceful refusal to be bullied and dominated. It is a neat and **ironic** twist in the **plot** that a repetition of this kind of injudicious interference with Darcy gives him the courage to propose to Elizabeth. Pride and prejudice are defeated at last, and by their own hand.

## M R AND MRS GARDINER

Elizabeth and Jane desperately need some reasonable relatives, if for nothing else to prove that their own good sense and behaviour is not a genetic impossibility. The Gardiners supply this role in the book. Surprisingly, the excellent Mr Gardiner is Mrs Bennet's brother. Austen wants to remind us that very near relatives do not necessarily share characteristics, and he is as different from his sister as, say, Elizabeth is from Lydia. Darcy takes to Mr Gardiner instantly at Pemberley, thereby proving his own lack of snobbery. He looks at the man and not the position in society. Mr Gardiner's home near Cheapside, in sight of his warehouses, was the source of much snobbish humour for Caroline Bingley. Darcy rises wholly above such views.

Mrs Gardiner is required as a wise adviser for the Bennet sisters, to compensate for the silliness of their mother. Elizabeth discusses the nature of Jane's love for Bingley with her (Chapter 25). She questions Elizabeth about her affection for Wickham (Chapters 26 and 27). Her letters and suggestions advance the plot: Jane stays with her in London; Elizabeth applies to her to learn why Darcy attended Lydia's wedding; the northern tour results in the fateful visit to Pemberley. Indeed it is a convenience of the plot that Mrs Gardiner should have been brought up near Pemberley, so as to make this a suitable place to visit when their visit to the Lakes falls through.

The Gardiners represent a happily married couple with children (four, boys and girls) in a book of bad marriages. They stand for decency, intelligence, good manners and kindness. According to the opinions presumed in Darcy at the start of the book, their position on the social scale should disallow them any such sophistication of behaviour. Clearly Austen shows a society in which the pride and prejudice of the landed gentry is being overthrown, and new definitions of social order are seen to triumph.

As characters they are somewhat sketchy. Mr Gardiner likes fishing, and Mrs Gardiner cannot walk very far – but both these traits are there to push the plot forward during the Pemberley visit by creating opportunities to meet Darcy. Throughout they have a vital place in the development of the narrative and the thematic structure of the book, but we do not learn very much about them.

## CHARLOTTE LUCAS

Is Charlotte Lucas wrong to have ensnared Mr Collins in marriage so swiftly and purposefully? The narrator stresses the deliberation of Charlotte's campaign. When she sees him walking towards the Lucas household, 'she instantly set out to meet him accidentally in the lane'. The narrator comments witheringly on Mr Collins's compliance: 'but little had she dared to hope that so much love and eloquence awaited her there'.

Elizabeth Bennet is astonished and mortified by Charlotte's agreement to marry Mr Collins. But what kind of future did Charlotte face had she not accepted Collins? Her brothers were 'relieved from their apprehension of Charlotte's dying an old maid' (Chapter 22).

At the crucial point in her argument for marrying Mr Collins in Chapter 22, concerning marriage as the 'only provision' for women in her position, it is not entirely clear whether the opinion being expressed is hers or the narrator's. There is nothing in *Pride and Prejudice* to contradict this statement.

Charlotte's only anxiety concerns Elizabeth's reaction to her decision. As she expects, Elizabeth is shocked. Charlotte is as knowing about Elizabeth's reaction to her marriage as she is about her own feelings in the matter, and she extracts a promise from Elizabeth to visit her in Kent. Chapters 28 and 30, which describe domestic life at Hunsford, must be read carefully to determine whether Charlotte's marriage is 'tolerable', or the misery that Elizabeth predicts. Certainly Mr Collins has not changed, and we see Charlotte humouring him with some skill. Likewise she has to suffer the interference of Lady Catherine with good grace. But Elizabeth has 'to give Charlotte credit for the arrangement' of rooms by which she sees relatively little of Mr Collins.

We have seen that Charlotte suspects Darcy's interest in Elizabeth (end of Chapter 32). Her 'eyes are open' on this matter, showing her powers of perception to be sharper than Elizabeth's. Clearly there is much that is irksome in Charlotte's life, but the narrator does not necessarily ask us to accept Elizabeth's view of events. In a novel where little is left to the reader's judgement, Austen seems to leave the question open as to Charlotte's 'happiness'. She certainly shows herself able to tolerate the disadvantages of her existence with dignity and kindness. She is entirely without self-pity. In Mr Collins's final letter to Mr Bennet (Chapter 57) we learn that she is pregnant. Does Elizabeth's beauty and wit, and their consequent advantages in the marriage market, blind her to the necessities of Charlotte's situation, or are we led into sharing her easy sense of superiority to her 'very plain' but honest friend? There is a pragmatic and self-interested aspect to love and marriage from which Elizabeth is not wholly immune. Charlotte shows this pragmatic view in her assessment of Elizabeth's attitude to Darcy: 'in her opinion it admitted not of a doubt, that all her friend's dislike would vanish, if she could suppose him to be in her power' (Chapter 32). She is wrong in the short term: Elizabeth refuses Darcy. And in the long term Elizabeth's love for Darcy grows in proportion to her feeling he has escaped 'her power'. But the end of the novel shows Charlotte to have been at least partially right.

## COLONEL FITZWILLIAM

Darcy's cousin, as an eligible man, offers a parallel and contrast to all the other eligible men in *Pride and Prejudice*. He is more immediately charming than Darcy, less apparently charming than Wickham, and, as a younger brother, not wealthy like Bingley. Above all he is an honest broker, totally trusted by Elizabeth, who can vouch for the truth of Darcy's letter. In Chapter 33 Elizabeth has a most interesting conversation with him. Firstly they discuss money in a dispassionate way: Colonel Fitzwilliam admits without rancour, that 'there are not many in my rank of life who can afford to marry without some attention to money'. His comments, and Elizabeth's teasing query about 'what is the usual price of an Earl's younger son' represent one aspect of the book's anti-romantic examination of the financial basis of marriage. Secondly Colonel Fitzwilliam inadvertently provides the vital proof that Darcy did indeed lure Bingley away from Jane: in the very next chapter she uses this information against him in anger.

## Sisters

*Pride and Prejudice* is a novel about sisters other than the Bennets.

Bingley has two sisters. **Mrs Hurst** is a cipher; we presume that her husband, whose chief interest is food, has married her for her money. His other sister **Caroline Bingley** enters into the **plot** as a false friend to Jane and a rival to Elizabeth in Darcy's affections, though Darcy appears to feel nothing but polite contempt for her advances. She participates in all the conversations at Netherfield, when Darcy is forming an agreeable impression of Elizabeth. In these she stands for snobbery, flattery of Darcy (as opposed to Elizabeth's wit and detachment) and jealousy. She offers a parallel and contrast to Elizabeth in their modes of conversation and courtship (since all conversations between unmarried men and women seem to involve an element of flirtation, grave or frivolous according to the persons involved). Though she had encouraged Jane to visit Netherfield, she decides that her brother must be detached from Jane (and Elizabeth kept away from Darcy), and so she is instrumental in Bingley's sudden departure from Hertfordshire.

Jane wants to believe in Caroline Bingley as a friend, but receives the cold shoulder from her in London, and has to admit that Elizabeth's cynical view of her behaviour has proved correct (in her letter in Chapter 26).

**Georgiana Darcy** is required in the novel's plot for a number of reasons. Caroline Bingley wants her brother to marry her, or this idea is offered as an obstacle to Jane's love for Bingley. Georgiana's near elopement with Wickham implicates Darcy in Lydia's elopement. Darcy's desire to introduce Georgiana to Elizabeth when they meet at Pemberley is a strong compliment and a clear indication of respect. Georgiana herself is characterised as shy, and her shyness is mistaken for pride: is this a hint at Darcy's character? Finally Georgiana's almost fearful respect for her brother is contrasted with Elizabeth's playful wifely behaviour in the final summing-up of the plot.

**Maria Lucas** is a foil for Elizabeth in their visit to Charlotte at Hunsford. Her innocent awe at the grandeur of Lady Catherine and Rosings and her ordinary interest in the domestic affairs of her sister, is a contrast to Elizabeth's self-reliance and sophistication, and perhaps her cynicism.

## SERVANTS

Servants in *Pride and Prejudice* are more characterised by their silence and anonymity than their explicit presence in the text, but the modern reader needs to be reminded that they are always there in the dining and drawing rooms of every house, as witnesses to the action. In Longbourn, a relatively modest household, the following servants are mentioned: the housekeeper, two housemaids, a butler and a footman. But there would probably have been more in such a household, and of course there were all the agricultural workers required on the estate, as well as managing the horses and carriage. Sometimes the knowledge of servants is a source of embarrassment, as, for example, the news of Lydia's elopement: ' "Oh, Jane!" cried Elizabeth, "was there a servant … who did not know the whole story by the end of the day?" ' (Chapter 47).

The housekeepers of Longbourn and Pemberley are mentioned by name (Mrs Hill and Mrs Reynolds), and they play a small part in the **plot**. Mrs Reynolds provides a surprising view of Darcy's good temper and absolute honour. Though the Gardiners and Elizabeth start by feeling that her views are the exaggerations of a fond old retainer, they are finally convinced that her admiration for Darcy is in fact a true witness to his true character: 'What praise is more valuable than the intelligent praise of a servant?' (Chapter 43). Mrs Hill is indispensable during the crisis of Lydia's disappearance, when Mrs Bennet takes to her bed in despairing hysterics; we can only imagine what might be her view of the Bennet household, and its master and mistress.

Only the ill-behaved Lydia shows any interest in the appearance of servants, and this seems to be a strong indication of her lack of decorum: 'that is just like your formality and discretion. You thought the waiter must not hear, as if he cared! I dare say he often hears worse things than I am going to say. But he is an ugly fellow! I am glad he is gone. I never saw such a long chin in my life' (Chapter 39).

# LOCATIONS

Austen writes with a careful sense of location – the reader always knows in what room of what house the action is taking place – but as with her characters, there is often surprisingly little detailed description. An exception to this is the guided tour round Pemberley and its park in Chapter 43, but of course this is to show exactly how wealthy and special Darcy is. There are three essential locations, in Hertfordshire, in Kent and in Derbyshire, and having a strong sense of these helps to master the plot. Events also take place in Brighton and London, but these happen 'off-stage' so to speak, and are reported by participants.

**Meryton** is a small town in Hertfordshire. It has a variety of shops and is big enough to hold the occasional 'public assembly'. The Bennet's house, called **Longbourn** after the village in which it is the main building, is one mile from Meryton. This is their only property; the Bennets do not have a winter residence in London. Three miles from Longbourn is **Netherfield Park**, rented by Bingley; this distance is considered an easy walk for men and robust young women, notably Elizabeth, though Bingley usually makes the journey on horseback, as does Jane (in the rain). The Lucas and Philips families all live within walking distance from each other and the Bennets in the environs of Meryton.

**Hunsford** in Kent is the village of which Mr Collins is the vicar. The Parsonage shares one of its boundaries with **Rosings Park**, the magnificent home of Lady Catherine de Bourgh and her daughter Anne. In Chapter 32 Elizabeth and Darcy disagree as to whether the fifty miles between Meryton and Hunsford is an 'easy distance' or not. For Darcy, 'fifty miles of good road' is 'little more than half a day's journey'; she points out that travel is expensive, and only the wealthy can consider such a distance easy.

**Pemberley House** in Derbyshire is a 'large, handsome, stone building', in a huge estate with its own woods and a river running through it. The park is ten miles round. Darcy spends about half the year there, the rest of the time in London. Five miles away is the village of **Lambton**, where Mrs Gardiner was brought up.

All the houses referred to above have their own land and gardens. Whenever the characters wish to be on their own, or discuss matters privately, they find a suitable spot outside. Thus Elizabeth has her 'favourite haunt' in the park of Rosings when she is staying in Kent (Chapter 33), where Darcy finds her to hand over his letter. Lady Catherine on her visit to Longbourn, chooses 'a prettyish kind of wilderness on one side of your lawn' (Chapter 56) as a suitably private spot in which to berate Elizabeth about her relationship with Darcy.

# THEMES AND CRITICAL ISSUES

In contemplating the action of her novel, Austen asks us to consider many questions about manners and morals:

- Whose behaviour is right?
- How should a gentleman behave?
- How should parents behave towards their children?
- How should children behave towards their parents?
- Should a woman make it clear she has fallen in love with a man?
- Is pride always wrong or sometimes justified?
- Who discovers and faces up to their own mistakes?
- Who is capable of changing themselves for the better, and who cannot change?

Some of the debates arising from the action of the story are examined in the discussion of characterisation above, as well as the sections devoted to individual characters; others are spelled out in the sections on **themes** and **motifs** below.

## CHARACTER AS A THEME

In the paragraphs above, the word 'character' is used in two ways: firstly to mean one of the imaginary persons who populate a novel; and secondly to refer to an individual's personality, that bundle of attitudes and behaviours that make us different from each other. An interest in this psychological individuality is touched upon at various points in the novel. 'I did not know before,' Bingley says to Elizabeth, 'that you were a studier of character. It must be an amusing study' (Chapter 9). Darcy asks her why she is asking so many questions: 'merely to the illustration of your character,' she replies, 'I am trying to make it out' (Chapter 18). The complaisant and easy-going Bingley is easily understood. Darcy however is 'intricate'.

During her rebuttal of Darcy's proposal, Elizabeth offers a comment on 'character' that suggests a rudimentary psychology that may help us in considering some of the characters in the book. Her anger is sparked off by Darcy's tactless account of his efforts to avoid falling in love with her: 'you chose to tell me that you liked me against your will, against your reason, and even against your character' (Chapter 34). This is a traditional view, opposing 'will' against 'reason': we are pulled in one direction by our desires, but we moderate them by our reason. 'Character' Elizabeth suggests is a separate entity. Her qualifying 'character' with 'even' suggests that Darcy has more control over this element in his make-up than over his will or reason. This suggests that 'character' is the deliberate, self-conscious and observable manner with which Darcy deals with the world. 'Character' would seem to be the collection of choices that an individual makes in the constant battle between desire and rational compromise. It is not simply 'manners': Wickham's manner may be perfect but his actions reveal his real character.

Often in Jane Austen's novels we are shown individuals overcoming powerful feelings. Elizabeth is shown on several occasions battling with herself, moderating her feelings by the processes of thinking rationally about them, or realising truths that she has formerly denied. Her response and steady change of attitude when she receives Darcy's letter is a notable example of this. Having preened herself on her ability to understand characters, she is furious when she finds herself to be entirely in the wrong with regard to Darcy and Wickham: 'I, who have prided myself on my discernment … How humiliating is this discovery! … I have courted prepossession and ignorance, and driven reason away … Till this moment, I never knew myself (Chapter 36).

We may consider Austen's range of characterisation in terms of this struggle between will and reason, desire and sense, and the realisation of truths. Some characters are the victims of their feelings and desires. Lydia, for example, simply follows her will. Her behaviour is untempered by reason or reasonableness: her morals and manners are deplorable. Mrs Bennet is completely the victim of her immediate feelings, which simply flow through her conversation unchecked.

It is plainly wrong to be the victim of one's feelings, and it seems a sign of excellence to be involved in the battles to control and understand themselves of the kind that Darcy and Elizabeth undergo. However *Pride and Prejudice* seems to argue that to possess these strong feelings in the first place is also creditable. Jane and Bingley nearly lose each other because Jane conceals her feelings, and Bingley can be persuaded to leave her by Darcy and his sisters. Mr Bennet's feelings and moral convictions are lost in the play of his **irony** and cynicism.

## PRIDE AND PREJUDICE

These are the explicit **themes** that Austen chooses to place as the title of her novel. Austen writes at a point of social change, and one area in which pride is seen to prevail is in the differences of class and wealth between characters. *Pride and Prejudice* shows how the ancient families of land-owning gentry are having to come to terms with new, mobile, wealthy middle-class families whose fortunes have been made by trade. Some, like Lady Catherine de Bourgh, cannot accept the way in which new class boundaries are having to be drawn. Darcy's marriage to Elizabeth Bennet will result in a link between her family and Wickham, but it is Wickham's origins as much as his bad character that makes her furious at this possibility. 'I am no stranger to the particulars of your youngest sister's infamous elopement … is *such* a girl to be my nephew's sister? Is *her* husband, is the son of his late father's steward, to be his brother? … Are the shades of Pemberley to be thus polluted?' (Chapter 56).

Mr Collins has absorbed Lady Catherine's vision of the world and is proud to be associated with her in every respect. It is noticeable how

the narrator suggests nothing but contempt for these two persons, who
are demeaned as **caricatures**. They are shown as unwaveringly and
ludicrously proud and stupid.

Darcy is proud. Charlotte Lucas, often the mouthpiece for
interesting opinions at odds with Elizabeth's, remarks that his pride:
'does not offend *me* so much as pride often does, because there is an
excuse for it … If I may so express it, he has a *right* to be proud' (Chapter
5). Darcy himself says that: 'where there is a real superiority of mind,
pride will always be under good regulation' (Chapter 11), which makes
Elizabeth smile, because she thinks his pride unregulated. The novel as a
whole shows Darcy learning to regulate his pride appropriately, and to
recognise that Elizabeth is not irredeemably tainted by the Bennet
family's social position and behaviour. He must also learn to bury these
prejudices when he addresses himself to Elizabeth.

The novel also shows us Elizabeth coming to terms with her
prejudice against Darcy. She makes up her mind about him too quickly,
based on his rude and stand-offish behaviour at the first dance at which
he appears in Meryton, when he remarks that 'she is not handsome
enough to tempt *me*' (Chapter 3). Elizabeth's first impressions lead her
astray. In her misjudgement of Wickham's character, she is taken in by
his handsome appearance. The novel teaches us that the ordinary human
prejudice in favour of a handsome appearance and a charming manner is
not to be trusted.

## MARRIAGE AND LOVE

There are four courtships leading up to marriage in the course of *Pride
and Prejudice* for the reader to consider, as well as two marriages which
are opened up to our scrutiny.

Charlotte Lucas and Mr Collins are the first 'lovers' to arrive at
marriage in the novel. Charlotte's reasons for marrying the nincompoop
Collins are explained in the section on her character above. Charlotte's
life at Hunsford poses the question: what is the nature of a 'successful'
marriage?

Lydia and Wickham start by living together. His interest in Lydia
is sexual; she is infatuated by his appearance. Both are shamelessly
uncaring about the disgrace that their immorality has caused the Bennet

family. Wickham is persuaded into marriage by a financial package. Austen presents their union as a model for a bad marriage, characterised by lack of love, integrity and money. We are not told that they have any children.

Jane and Bingley represent the coming-together of two handsome, like-minded and kind-hearted persons. Their eventual marriage is delightful but a bit wishy-washy. It is doubtful that their separation, for which in the weakness of their characters and love they are partly responsible, has deepened their understanding of themselves or each other. But since they are so well matched this scarcely matters.

Elizabeth and Darcy have to overcome his pride and her disdainful dislike of him in order to realise their love. In doing this they both change considerably, and they have to learn hard lessons about their own inadequacies of character and understanding. But they also learn about each other and their respective qualities in times of stress. Theirs is a marriage of opposites. Her liveliness and mischievous pleasure in the oddities of human behaviour is combined with his self-conscious gravity and decency. This mutual knowledge, the pattern of the novel suggests, makes their marriage the strongest and most interesting of all.

The Bennets' marriage is shown to us throughout the novel, and is explained by the narrator late on in the narrative, at the start of Chapter 42. It is a picture of a bad marriage: 'respect, esteem and confidence, had vanished for ever'. When Mr Bennet questions Elizabeth at length about her true feelings for Darcy, he shows true responsibility, and a sense of the pain behind his **irony** emerges: 'my child, let me not have the grief of seeing *you* unable to respect your partner in life' (Chapter 59).

The Gardiners are an amiable couple with a brood of lively children. The novel ends with a compliment to them, as the persons who by bringing Elizabeth to Derbyshire had brought her and Darcy together. This is true in terms of the plot, but in a larger way the Gardiners illustrate the benefits and blessings of marriage itself. The institution of marriage, to which all the characters in the novel devote themselves with relative success or failure, is upheld by the Gardiners. The happiness of a wise marriage is perhaps the 'truth universally acknowledged' that hovers over *Pride and Prejudice*. For Austen and her sensible characters, nothing matters more.

Love in *Pride and Prejudice* often has to do with marriage. The novel shows it to be a state of rhapsodical admiration into which young men pass before making their proposals: Darcy does this twice, Bingley once, while Mr Collins pays lip service to the state of mind without having been affected.

Austen depicts love as usually a secret, internalised, almost shameful state of mind: the victims above start by expressing admiration and liking, but then have to blurt the word out. As in Elizabeth's love for Darcy, it can be concealed from everyone, even from her closest family and friends. Jane, her confidante in everything, is astonished to hear of it. The object of such feeling is often in a state of ignorance too, as Bingley is of Jane's love for him. Charlotte believes it useful to display these feelings so as to leave no one in doubt. The events of the novel suggest there might have been wisdom in this view for Jane and Elizabeth. In Charlotte's own case there is no love for Mr Collins to conceal, but she is equally open and active in her agreement to his business arrangement.

Trying to spot where people's affections really lie is a pastime indulged by many characters in the book. Mrs Gardiner warns Elizabeth about her growing attachment to Wickham and later looks in vain for clues to her feelings towards Darcy. Caroline Bingley ruthless teases Darcy about his admiration for Elizabeth's 'fine eyes'.

Unrequited love, like Jane's for Bingley, is an undesirable state of mind in itself – we feel nothing but sympathy for Jane. Things are worse if it is a matter of public knowledge, as it is for Jane. Elizabeth keeps her growing interest in Darcy secret with good reason.

Much of the comedy of the novel involves the mismatch of feeling between lovers, and the misunderstandings caused by their public appearance and the private reality of their feelings. It is ironic that Darcy takes Bingley away from Jane because he thinks she is not in love with him (while Bingley is falling in love with her), and then himself proposes to Elizabeth when she detests him.

Whatever we are to call Lydia's feelings for Wickham, they do not legitimise her actions. They are shown to be too much bound up with Wickham's appearance, and not at all interested in his true character behind that appearance. Lydia is prepared to live with him unmarried, though in running away with him, she has every chance to see him for what he really is.

## MONEY AND SELF-INTEREST

Charlotte Collins, thinking up 'kind schemes' for Elizabeth, feels that Colonel Fitzwilliam was 'beyond comparison the pleasantest man; he certainly admired her, and his situation in life was most eligible; but, to counterbalance these advantages, Mr Darcy had considerable patronage in the church and his cousin could have none at all' (Chapter 32). Placing this at the end of a chapter emphasises the final twist, in which Charlotte's thoughts move from the outcome that might suit her friend best, to that which would serve her own purposes through the advancement and enrichment of Mr Collins. We are tempted into laughing at the way Charlotte's fanciful speculations come down to earth in self-interest.

Charlotte remarks of herself 'I am not romantic you know' (Chapter 22). Neither is the narrator of *Pride and Prejudice*. This is a love story, but one in which passion is tempered by sensible thoughts about money. Lydia is not unpassionate in her admiration for Wickham. In some novels to throw caution to the winds and run away with a handsome young officer would be the very emblem of thrillingly passionate behaviour. In this novel it is severely condemned. The financial fecklessness of Wickham is as strong a mark against him as his sexual immorality.

So careful is the narrator to give financial details of almost every significant character in *Pride and Prejudice*, that money almost amounts to a **theme**. Details of their respective incomes and capital are provided in the list of characters.

When Elizabeth comments to Jane, that her love for Darcy began 'from my first seeing his beautiful grounds at Pemberley' (Chapter 59), what element of truthfulness is there in this? She feels 'some perturbation' on approaching Pemberley: 'her spirits were in a high flutter' (Chapter 43). When she sees the estate (the only piece of sustained topographical description in the book, and therefore **foregrounded**), 'at that moment she felt, that to be mistress of Pemberley might be something!' She speaks of a present and a future, not of something past and concluded. It is not 'to have been' but 'to be'. Darcy's wealth is of great interest to Elizabeth, when she is confronted by its reality.

The females of the Bennet family are in real financial difficulty. When Mr Bennet dies, they lose their home and the income attached to it. Even a stickler for old ways like Lady Catherine regards the entailment of property down through male relatives, excluding wives and daughters, to be unnecessary (not least because it would have deprived her of Rosings). There is a hard and unsentimental reality to almost every aspect of this comedy of courtship and marriage.

## Luck and happiness

Inherent in the **plot** of *Pride and Prejudice* is a debate about the nature of luck. There is a pattern of circumstances and events that is outside the control of the characters, but which is essential in the furthering of the narrative. It is good luck that Mrs Gardiner was brought up near Pemberley, that Mr Gardiner's business interests curtail the time available for the proposed Lake District tour so that Elizabeth and the Gardiners visit Derbyshire, and that Darcy should return to Pemberley earlier than expected and therefore bump into Elizabeth. None of these events in themselves stretches our credulity too far. All is realistic and likely, and Austen is not suggesting anything providential or mystical in the bringing together of the would-be lovers. Indeed the motive for the visit is Mrs Gardiner's (and eventually Elizabeth's) very strong curiosity to see round the house and grounds. Nonetheless an implicit suggestion in this arrangement is that chance plays a strong part in human fortune. In an argument on a different subject, Charlotte Lucas remarks that 'happiness in marriage is entirely a matter of chance' (Chapter 6), and the plot of the novel demonstrates that chance certainly plays its part in bringing a solution to the apparent stalemate in the marital hopes of the two Bennet sisters.

## Women's role

To what degree does Austen specifically address the issues facing women in the society she depicts in her novels? This is a question which many critics have addressed in the last twenty-five years and to which a variety of answers have been put forward. There is plenty of evidence to consider in *Pride and Prejudice*.

It is a woman's perception of events that we are shown: it is a commonplace of Austen criticism that men are never shown away from the company of women. We are shown sisters, aunts and female confidantes exchanging views, discussing events and sharing secrets. In the course of these discussions, and in the unfolding events of the novel, many different points of view about marriage are expressed, from Mrs Bennet's obsessive planning to Mr Bennet's disdainful **irony**. But as argued above, the nature of a good marriage seems the book's major **theme**, and it does not present in a positive light any possible role for educated young women other than marriage. At the novel's end, Mary Bennet seems to be heading for an unmarried life looking after her mother, but her character and learning are not rendered admirable during the book. Indeed the narrator suggests somewhat cruelly that her studies were a strategy to make up for her lack of beauty.

In Chapter 8 there is a discussion of the 'accomplishments' of young ladies. Bingley is all admiration for their ability to 'paint tables, cover skreens and net purses'. Darcy wants more than this, and more even than the list Caroline Bingley provides of 'music, singing, drawing, dancing and the modern languages', plus 'something in her air and manner of walking'. To all these Darcy adds 'the improvement of her mind by extensive reading'. We know nothing of Elizabeth's reading, though Darcy attempts to draw her into discussing books at the Netherfield ball. She can sing and play the piano, but, to Lady Catherine's astonishment, does not draw. What the novel presents is Elizabeth's independence of mind and the spirited freedom of her thinking about her world, even in spite of the pressures caused by its narrowness, snobbery and the straitjacket of its conventions. Darcy calls this 'liveliness of mind' and she brands it 'impudence' when at the book's end they look back on their early conversations: 'you were sick of civility, of deference, of officious attention. You were disgusted with the women who were always speaking and looking, and thinking of *your* approbation alone. I roused, and interested you, because I was so unlike *them*' (Chapter 60). Elizabeth may be put forward as a role model for female readers, but she is a hard act to imitate, as her desirability rests in her intelligence and charisma, rather than any set of accomplishments that can be learnt.

Elizabeth controls the conversations at Netherfield, and always dominates Darcy in conversation, often drawing attention to his broody silences. She tells her father in vain that Lydia should be controlled. She stands up to Lady Catherine. She breaks the silence between herself and Darcy by thanking him for his secret generosity to Lydia. Within the limits of her situation she is an extremely strong young woman. But her strength does not go beyond the conventional propriety of a daughter and wife; duty to family and husband remains central to the female agenda.

## NARROWNESS OF VISION

The scope of *Pride and Prejudice* requires comment. The narrowness of Jane Austen's interests as a novelist has been a source both of criticism and praise. She described her material herself in letters: '3 or 4 Families in a Country Village is the very thing to work on' (to Anna Austen, September 1814). In another description she uses an image of miniaturist painting, a 'little bit (two Inches wide) of Ivory on which I work with so fine a brush' (to J. Edward Austen, 16 December 1816). From within this narrow framework, we see nothing of the agricultural year, the running of the households, the poverty or otherwise of ordinary villagers. There is no vivid sense of a wider world than Meryton, Hunsford and Pemberley. The Gardiners live in London, but it is merely a place that has to be crossed, and where Wickham can hide easily.

The Bennets and their acquaintances seem to be protected from the tides of history. The arrival of the militia in Meryton hints at political events, in fact war with Napoleon, but this is not explained or dwelt upon.

Some readers have found this apparent littleness of subject matter claustrophobic and unambitious. Various strategies can be adopted to counter this criticism. One is to claim that within the world that Austen describes we are shown all the range of good and wicked human behaviour. Another is to scour the novels for references to the political events of the time, and recuperate (or vilify) Austen by suggesting her attitudes to the politics of the early nineteenth century.

Others see the restrictions of Austen's chosen subject matter as a source of strength and exactitude. One of Austen's early admirers was Sir Walter Scott, a novelist who took on the largest themes of history and politics: rereading *Pride and Prejudice* he remarks in his *Journal* on Austen's 'talent for describing the involvements, and feelings, and characters of ordinary life, which is to me the most wonderful I ever met with. The Big Bow-wow strain I can do myself like any now going; but the exquisite touch, which renders ordinary commonplace things and characters interesting, from the truth of the description, and the sentiment, is denied to me' (14 March 1826).

A truism of recent criticism is that all writing is political. Therefore whether explicitly or not, Austen shows through her language a set of values and assumptions about the world she describes which amounts to a political agenda. Critics can then argue as to whether Austen's novels reveal an innate conservatism and unthinking support for the political and social status quo, or whether there is a subtle proto-feminism in her depiction of women struggling to achieve independence of mind in a world ruled by weak men. There is further discussion of this debate in the section on Critical History and Broader Perspectives.

## THE IMPLIED READER

From the evidence of the text itself, is it possible to work out the kind of reader that Austen had in mind for *Pride and Prejudice*? Clearly we are supposed to be able to identify with the Bennet sisters and their predicament. Assumptions are made about its readership both in what the novel provides, and also in what it leaves out as not worth explaining. Novel reading relies on a certain level of leisure, and leisure was a rare commodity till industrialisation resulted in the Factory Acts from 1833 onwards that formalised working hours and holidays. The main characters in the novel are members of this elite leisured class: indeed none of them are seen working, or appear burdened by work at all (except Mr Gardiner). Pemberley seems to run itself, though the number of letters that Darcy must have to write to pursue the business of his estate is a subject for Caroline Bingley's admiration. Work is not an option for the young women depicted. They are, however, surrounded by female servants who have no option but to work. Austen seems to accept this social situation as natural and just.

# Narrative techniques

## The narrator

*Pride and Prejudice* is told to us by an anonymous and **omniscient narrator**. Sometimes the narrator is the silent observer of events, relating them without comment. At other times we are told quite clearly what to think about a character or an incident. An obvious feature of the narrative are those passages of summary, often at the beginning or the end of a chapter, when the narrator takes command and offers opinions or sums up aspects of the characters. These are sharply different in tone and **style** from passages that describe the incidents and events of the novel. Often the difference lies in the way in which time is handled. The moving present of the action is described as it happens, while reflections that depart from this moving present involve the narrator generalising or going back in time or summarising a passage of time.

A narrator who summarises and comments (not all narrators do this: some try to be entirely anonymous) to some extent has the same kind of existence for us as a character in the novel. In some novels – though not in this one – we come to regard the narrative voice as less than completely trustworthy. We have to stand back and see that the way the story is being told is partial or from a particular and limited perspective. There are examples of a partial view of events in *Pride and Prejudice*, but not to the extent that we would regard the narrator as unreliable. For example, we are not immediately told all we need to know about Darcy and Wickham's past to know that Elizabeth is judging the merit of these two men quite wrongly. If we had known this, then we could have enjoyed knowingly watching her make her mistakes, rather than learning from events as she does. To this extent the narrator enjoys mildly tricking her readers.

*Her* readers: it would be perverse to call the narrator *he*. But for the purposes of discussing all the effects of the text, we should not simply assume that this narrator *is* Jane Austen. Is there any aspect of the text that would mark the narrator as female? She has a sharp (and critical) eye for an interest in female fashion, though little is said about the clothes themselves. She is equally clear-sighted about carriages, and money (but then so are many of the women in the book). She seems to despise many of the female characters' foibles, some of which might be regarded as gender specific. But she is equally harsh on the inadequacy and pomposity of her male characters. The spheres of activity in the novel are those in which women are always present. Men are never shown outside the company of women. It might be argued that the main **theme** of the novel, marriage, suggests a female perspective; but of course men are equally involved in the business of wedlock, and they have much to learn from the male mistakes that are perpetrated in the novel.

The narrator selects the incidents we see and finds the words to describe them. There is no sense of things unfolding chaotically in Austen's novels. We sense from the first pages of the text that she knows where events are leading, and that everything we are being told or shown may be significant and somehow related to the final outcome of events. This strong impression of control and her capacity to judge and mock her characters suggests the presence of someone highly intelligent, who is impatient with the follies of human nature.

In her summaries the narrator is judgemental. She sometimes mocks her characters. This places her above the comic world she describes. Her summarising authorial comment on characters can be ferociously direct and critical – Mrs Bennet's ignorance for example at the end of the first chapter.

As the novel develops, we tend to be shown events from Elizabeth's point of view, using her as a **centre of consciousness**. We do witness conversations in which she does not participate, for example when Bingley's sisters comment on her appearance behind her back in Chapter 8. And even towards the end of the novel, the narrator will tell us quite unexpectedly what another character, such as Mrs Gardiner, is thinking. However, large stretches of the novel are given over to the attempt to reproduce the contents of Elizabeth's consciousness as she modifies her view of Darcy from settled dislike to love. One of the narrative techniques used to achieve this is **free indirect discourse** (Oh! Why did she come (chapter 45)), which is mid-way between direct speech or thought (Oh! Why did I come?), and reported speech or thought (she wondered why she had come). Free indirect thought is used throughout the novel and suggests Austen's determination to display the psychological processes of her **protagonist**

## IRONY

The narrator loves to make **ironic** comments about some of her characters. In Chapter 22, Charlotte Lucas is worried that Mr Collins will have to depart from Hertfordshire before her scheme can succeed: 'but here, she did injustice to the *fire and independence of his character*, for it led him to escape out of Longbourn House the next morning with admirable slyness, and hasten to Lucas Lodge *to throw himself at her feet*' (italics added). Such fire and passion, though hackneyed, is the opposite of all that we know of Mr Collins, and we take pleasure in the inappropriateness of the description. The narrator may be indicating the language that Mr Collins might himself use to aggrandise his activities, but the effect is still ironically amusing. We know that we are not to accept the description at its face value.

Occasionally Elizabeth indulges in malicious irony. ' "*I like her appearance*" ', she says on seeing Miss De Bourgh for the first time, but then she explains what is so pleasing: ' "she looks sickly and cross.—Yes, she will do very well for him" ' (italics added, Chapter 28).

In irony of this kind, we need to know something that lies outside the immediate sentence in order to understand what is meant. In the first case we have to know Mr Collins for the calculating and pompous ass that he is, to understand that the description of his actions is inappropriate. In the second, we soon learn Elizabeth does not like Miss De Bourgh's appearance at all, except in so far as it fuels her dislike for Darcy. The danger of saying something that you do not mean is that unless your audience shares your point of view, they may miss the point entirely. As readers we have to be perpetually on our guard to pick up the ironies, or miss the point.

Examples so far have shown irony as a feature of language, but irony can be as much a way of thinking as a technique. The word 'ironic' is used to describe the ability to see things from several points of view. In this respect Austen's writing is always ironic. She likes to present mutually incompatible points of view. This is true of her treatment of her largest **themes** and incidents. A central irony of the novel is that Darcy proposes to Elizabeth, who detests him.

The narrator shares an ironic enjoyment of the activities of her characters with Mr Bennet and with Elizabeth. Mr Bennet's irony is constant and public. Elizabeth rarely exercises her irony in this way at the expense of others, and where she exercises irony in public, it is in the form of a playful conversational exchange, part of her love for **paradox**, rather than as a way of indulging in the superiority of private detachment. Darcy is the chief butt of this kind of wit, and he is intelligent enough to know the nature of Elizabeth's game, and follow the play of her ideas, even when he is under attack.

## LETTERS

*Pride and Prejudice* contains some forty letters, their contents reported or reproduced in their entirety. Many of the eighteenth-century English novels that Austen read, such as Samuel Richardson's *Clarissa* (1748), or Fanny Burney's *Evelina* (1778) are **epistolary novels**, consisting entirely of letters. Such a method of writing a novel was not at all unusual in the early nineteenth century. *First Impressions*, the lost original of *Pride and Prejudice*, was constructed in this way. In *Pride and Prejudice* letters are part of the text's verisimilitude. They feel authentic.

Letter writing is a serious business for characters like Darcy, Jane, and Mr and Mrs Gardiner. Alternatively, Lydia's effusions are skimpy and trivial or shamelessly venal, as in her application for money in the last chapter. Mr Bennet is a lazy letter-writer; his are infrequent and short. Letters provide a way of distinguishing character. Mr Collins is recognised as a buffoon from his first letter. Darcy's letter of explanation to Elizabeth is a crucial text in itself: 'she was in a fair way of soon knowing it by heart. She studied every sentence: and her feelings towards its writer were at times widely different' (Chapter 37). Anyone who doubts the variety of Austen's capacities as a writer should compare the different styles of the letters in *Pride and Prejudice*.

## STYLE AND LANGUAGE

Jane Austen's **style** seems more reminiscent of the prose-writers of the eighteenth century than that of the romantic poets who were her contemporaries. There are very few descriptive passages. What is in the text is there for a purpose: there is no painting in words, no description for its own sake.

There are indeed relatively few **concrete nouns** in *Pride and Prejudice*. A few objects spring to mind – carriages, a muddy petticoat, several hats, pictures, a parasol, pyramids of grapes, nectarines and peaches that provide a welcome distraction during an embarrassing social occasion. Such things that are mentioned serve an immediate purpose. She is not interested in visualising the world she describes, expect in special cases, like Pemberley. This applies also to the appearance of her characters.

A far larger proportion of nouns in Austen's prose deal with abstractions and generalities, with ideas and feelings. Open any page and **abstract nouns** are almost everywhere: astonishment, pride, sense, judgement, hope, etc.

There is little or no **metaphor** in Pride and Prejudice. There is however one kind of **figurative language** which relates Austen to prose writers of the middle and late eighteenth century like Dr Johnson. This is the structuring of her sentences and arrangement of words so as to create a sense of balance, pattern and proportion. In the following case, the linguistic cleverness is ascribed to Elizabeth, who is thinking about Charlotte: 'her home, and her housekeeping, her parish and her poultry, and all their dependent concerns, had not yet lost their charms' (Chapter 38). The alliteration draws attention to the two pairs of words. 'Home' and 'housekeeping' fit together well, though the first suggests positive, warm values, the second concerns money and work. 'Parish' widens the concerns away from the parsonage to a wider scope of responsibility, but 'poultry' rather than finishing the list with a final grand idea, ends on a note of **bathos**; by the **antithesis** between these ideas, Charlotte's concerns are finally condemned as narrow and trivial.

# REALISM

Given that in *Pride and Prejudice* Austen is not interested in description for its own sake, and her vocabulary is distinguished by the predominance of abstract words, it is perhaps odd to insist that she her chosen mode of writing is **realism**. This has to do as much with the milieu and manners she chooses as her subject as the way in which she writes about them.

Meryton is recognisably an ordinary society not unlike that inhabited by her original readers. She does not describe a fantasy world. There are no haunted ruins, dungeons or castles; no mad monks or man-made monsters. In other words, this is not a gothic novel, in which the pleasure consists of entering a world quite unlike our own normally humdrum existence, where feelings and passions are stretched to excess, far beyond the key values of Austen's society: propriety, amiability, civility.

# PART FOUR

# Textual analysis

TEXT 1 (FROM CHAPTER 11)

'Mr. Darcy is not to be laughed at!' cried Elizabeth. 'That is an uncommon advantage, and uncommon I hope it will continue, for it would be a great loss to *me* to have many such acquaintance. I dearly love a laugh.'

'Miss Bingley,' said he [Darcy], 'has given me credit for more than can be. The wisest and the best of men, nay, the wisest and best of their actions, may be rendered ridiculous by a person whose first object in life is a joke.'

'Certainly,' replied Elizabeth — 'there are such people, but I hope I am not one of *them*. I hope I never ridicule what is wise or good. Follies and nonsense, whims and inconsistencies *do* divert me, I own, and I laugh at them whenever I can. — But these, I suppose, are precisely what you are without.'

'Perhaps that is not possible for anyone. But it has been the study of my life to avoid those weaknesses which often expose a strong understanding to ridicule.'

'Such as vanity and pride.'

'Yes, vanity is a weakness indeed. But pride — where there is a real superiority of mind, pride will be always under good regulation.'

Elizabeth turned away to hide a smile.

'Your examination of Mr. Darcy is over, I presume,' said Miss Bingley; — 'and pray what is the result?'

'I am perfectly convinced by it that Mr. Darcy has no defect. He owns it himself without disguise.'

'No' — said Darcy, 'I have made no such pretension. I have faults enough, but they are not, I hope, of understanding. My temper I dare vouch for. — It is I believe too little yielding — certainly too little for the convenience of the world. I cannot forget the follies and vices of others so soon as I ought, nor their offences against myself. My feelings are not puffed about with every attempt to move them. My temper would perhaps be called resentful. — My good opinion once lost is lost for ever.'

'*That* is a failing indeed!' — cried Elizabeth. 'Implacable resentment *is* a shade in a character. But you have chosen your fault well. — I really cannot *laugh* at it. You are safe from me.'

'There is, I believe, in every disposition a tendency to some particular evil, a natural defect, which not even the best education can overcome.'

'And *your* defect is a propensity to hate every body.'

'And yours,' he replied with a smile, 'is wilfully to misunderstand them.'

'Do let us have a little music,' — cried Miss Bingley, tired of a conversation in which she had no share. —'Louisa, you will not mind my waking Mr. Hurst.'

Her sister made not the smallest objection, and the piano forte was opened, and Darcy, after a few moments recollection, was not sorry for it. He began to feel the danger of paying Elizabeth too much attention.

Elizabeth Bennet is celebrated as a character for her lively wit and independence of mind, and this passage provides evidence for this view. Here, she is at Netherfield, where she is looking after her sister Jane. This is the evening of the second day spent there, so she is already familiar with the company. This is the last of several conversations which she and Darcy have covering a variety of topics, including reading, letter-writing, the pliancy of Bingley as a friend, and the desirable accomplishments for young women. As in most of these discussions, she and Darcy become sparring partners to the exclusion of the others, in this case Caroline Bingley. Caroline is beginning to feel that Elizabeth is interesting to Darcy, though he has not yet admitted to admiring her 'fine eyes', so her jealousy is still emerging, rather than rampant. Darcy himself has stung Elizabeth by calling her only 'tolerable' and, within the bounds of politeness, she is out to avenge this insult. Her assertion therefore that Darcy is beyond laughter is something of a taunt. Her comment is in answer to Caroline's refusal to tease Darcy: 'teaze calmness of temper and presence of mind. No, no ...'

This is a little drama of sexual attraction, which seems to be on everyone's mind whether they experience it or not. Austen captures the way Caroline does all she can to praise Darcy, and does not interest him, while Elizabeth does all she can to annoy him, and thereby is attractive to him. It is this rivalry between the two young women, deeply felt by

Caroline, but entered into light-heartedly by Elizabeth that is the **subtext** of the early discussion. Now the subtext changes, as Elizabeth brings her wit to bear on Darcy, whose pride has so annoyed her. Caroline is left out of the conversation – she eventually brings it to an end, piqued that things have got out of her control.

The subject of their exchange is of central interest in *Pride and Prejudice*. Who and what have we the right to laugh at? The novel adopts an **ironic** and **satiric** attitude to much of its material. Here the propriety of such a way of viewing things is discussed. Elizabeth asserts that it is uncommon for anyone to be laughter-proof. It is mildly **paradoxical** that she wants acquaintances that she can laugh at, as if she wants fools for friends. The implication is that everyone, even the present company, can be the butt of derision. Darcy replies with some gravity that anyone can be made to look ridiculous by a frivolous-minded person, by implication like Elizabeth. She offers a conventional defence of satire – hers is aimed only at human folly and she will never mock the wise and good. We may speculate that this is also the narrator's position. Then Elizabeth turns the conversation back against Darcy, by drawing from his comment the false conclusion that he is without fault. His reply, that he attempts to avoid weakness, is a bit pompous and feeble, and he emphasises his good qualities, his 'study' and his 'strong understanding'. Elizabeth delivers her *coup-de-grâce*: 'vanity and pride' is what she detests in Darcy and the present company. Given the title of the novel, the reader is alert to the implications of this attack. An explicit **theme** of the book, already broached in a number of preceding chapters (Mary's homily and Charlotte's comment in Chapter 5) is under discussion.

Darcy pronounces on his sense of superiority, in the following grave terms: 'vanity is a weakness indeed. But pride – where there is a real superiority of mind, pride will be always under good regulation'. He seems to change his mind in mid-sentence. The natural sequence of ideas after the 'but' is to say that pride is not a weakness: vanity is, but pride isn't. Alert to the trap she has laid, he states instead that it requires to be properly controlled. Indeed, his answer shows exactly such proper control. Elizabeth has to hide her triumph and amusement. She has found a way of attacking his vice.

Darcy seems to know he is under attack and his only defence is a reasonable seriousness; but it makes him sound pompous in contrast with

Elizabeth's lightness of thrust. But then he further traps himself in her conversational sparring by admitting to being 'resentful'. So now Elizabeth can chide him with the fault of 'implacable resentment', then exaggerated into 'a propensity to hate every body'. She has indeed found a 'shade' in his character. His riposte gracefully admits defeat.

Elizabeth is shown irrepressibly teasing Darcy's seriousness and self-importance. Rather than resenting the way she twists his comments, he is amused by her cleverness. He realises the 'danger' of conversation with someone of her wit and intelligence. The word 'danger' has already been used in this context in Chapter 10, and the repetition of this strong word, placed in such a significant position of the last sentence of the chapter, marks a further point in the development of Darcy's interest.

In Chapter 60 they discuss this phase in their relationship. Darcy admits he admired Elizabeth's 'liveliness of mind', which she calls 'impudence'. And she puts forward the view that it was her refusal to try to please him (implicitly, in the manner of Caroline Bingley) that made her attractive. Austen recognises the peculiar ways in which attraction and love function.

TEXT 2     (FROM CHAPTER 26)

'I am not likely to leave Kent for some time. Promise me, therefore, to come to Hunsford.'

Elizabeth could not refuse, though she foresaw little pleasure in the visit.

'My father and Maria are to come to me in March,' added Charlotte, 'and I hope you will consent to be of the party. Indeed, Eliza, you will be as welcome to me as either of them.'

The wedding took place; the bride and bridegroom set off for Kent from the church door, and every body had as much to say or to hear on the subject as usual. Elizabeth soon heard from her friend; and their correspondence was as regular and frequent as it had ever been; that it should be equally unreserved was impossible. Elizabeth could never address her without feeling that all the comfort of intimacy was over, and, though determined not to slacken as a correspondent, it was for the sake of what had been, rather than what was. Charlotte's first letters were received with a good deal of eagerness; there could not but be curiosity to know how she would speak of her new home, how she would like Lady Catherine, and how happy she would dare pronounce herself to be; though, when the letters were read, Elizabeth felt that Charlotte expressed herself on every point exactly as she might have foreseen. She wrote cheerfully, seemed surrounded with comforts, and mentioned nothing which she could not praise. The house, furniture, neighbourhood, and roads, were all to her taste, and Lady Catherine's behaviour was most friendly and obliging. It was Mr. Collins's picture of Hunsford and Rosings rationally softened; and Elizabeth perceived that she must wait for her own visit there, to know the rest.

Jane had already written a few lines to her sister to announce their safe arrival in London; and when she wrote again, Elizabeth hoped it would be in her power to say something of the Bingleys.

This is not a crucial or dramatic passage, but rather a piece of narratorial summary linking scenes and events. Information is provided about Elizabeth's view of Charlotte over a passage of time. It is a source of sadness that Elizabeth no longer feels friendship for Charlotte. She will still honour her promise to visit, and correspond, though this will be a matter of duty rather than pleasure.

Marriage is not depicted as always spelling the end of friendship between women, but marriage to Mr Collins is such a disastrous step in Elizabeth's view, that she cannot fully respect Charlotte's decision to pursue and accept him.

The passage is all about letters, and there are more letters in the rest of the chapter. It is easy to see traces of the lost original draft of *Pride and Prejudice*, which was in **epistolary** form. Austen often uses reference to letters when she wants to advance the action through time quite quickly.

The description of Charlotte's wedding is squeezed into a sentence: 'The wedding took place, the bride and bridegroom set off for Kent from the church door, and every body had as much to say or to hear on the subject as usual.' There is a distinction implied between those who have lots to say and those (less fortunate perhaps) who have to listen to them. Another pleasant opposition is between the suggested garrulity of the wedding guests and the narrator's short way of describing it.

In this case, 'every body' reminds us that in the background of the novel is constant talk, the 'news' that is Mrs Bennet's solace. Public opinion in the form of gossip is always something to contend with: 'the

Bennets were speedily pronounced to be the luckiest family in the world, though only a few weeks before, when Lydia had first run away, they had generally proved to be marked out for misfortune' (Chapter 55).

Here Charlotte's letters are shown to be part of Elizabeth's inner life; they inform her way of thinking about her friend, but they are curiously disappointing, though they deal with life in Hunsford in exactly the cheerful, 'rationally softened' way which Elizabeth would have expected from Charlotte. Only the visit to Hunsford will allow her to 'know the rest'. Does she want Charlotte to admit her mistake in marrying Mr Collins?

Movement from the public to the private, from a dramatised scene to Elizabeth's thought-processes, as in this passage, is a constant element in *Pride and Prejudice*. Elizabeth's reading of the letters allows a view of her consciousness that is different in effect, and less immediate, than the **free indirect style** used by Austen to reveal a character's thinking, often at moments of stress. Here we are shown a developing meditation on a topic over a period of time.

TEXT 3  (FROM CHAPTER 46)

'When *my* eyes were opened to his real character. — Oh! had I known what I ought, what I dared, to do! But I knew not — I was afraid of doing too much. Wretched, wretched, mistake!'

Darcy made no answer. He seemed scarcely to hear her, and was walking up and down the room in earnest meditation; his brow contracted, his air gloomy. Elizabeth soon observed, and instantly understood it. Her power was sinking; every thing *must* sink under such a proof of family weakness, such an assurance of the deepest disgrace. She could neither wonder nor condemn, but the belief of his self-conquest brought nothing consolatory to her bosom, afforded no palliation of her distress. It was, on the contrary, exactly calculated to make her understand her own wishes; and never had she so honestly felt that she could have loved him, as now, when all love must be vain.

But self, though it would intrude, could not engross her. Lydia — the humiliation, the misery, she was bringing on them all, soon swallowed up every private care; and covering her face with her handkerchief, Elizabeth was soon lost to every thing else; and, after a pause of several minutes, was only recalled to a sense of her situation by the voice of her companion, who, in a manner, which though it spoke compassion, spoke likewise restraint, said, 'I am afraid you have been long desiring my absence, nor have I any thing to plead in excuse of my stay, but real, though unavailing, concern. Would to heaven that any thing could be either said or done on my part, that might offer consolation to such distress. — But I will not torment you with vain wishes, which may seem purposely to ask for your thanks. This unfortunate affair will, I fear, prevent my sister's having the pleasure of seeing you at Pemberley to day.'

'Oh, yes. Be so kind as to apologize for us to Miss Darcy. Say that urgent business calls us home immediately. Conceal the unhappy truth as long as it is possible. — I know it cannot be long.'

He readily assured her of his secrecy — again expressed his sorrow for her distress, wished it a happier conclusion than there was at present reason to hope, and leaving his compliments for her relations, with only one serious, parting, look, went away.

As he quitted the room, Elizabeth felt how improbable it was that they should ever see each other again on such terms of cordiality as had marked their several meetings in Derbyshire; and as she threw a retrospective glance over the whole of their acquaintance, so full of contradictions and varieties, sighed at the perverseness of those feelings which would now have promoted its continuance, and would formerly have rejoiced in its termination.

If gratitude and esteem are good foundations of affection, Elizabeth's change of sentiment will be neither improbable nor faulty. But if otherwise, if the regard springing from such sources is unreasonable or unnatural, in comparison of what is so often described as arising on a first interview with its object, and even before two words have been exchanged, nothing can be said in her defence, except that she had given somewhat of a trial to the latter method, in her partiality for Wickham, and that its ill-success might perhaps authorise her to seek the other less interesting mode of attachment. Be that as it may, she saw him go with regret; and in this early example of what Lydia's infamy must produce, found additional anguish as she reflected on that wretched business.

There is nothing comic in the language of this passage, though the situation is full of heavy **irony**, perhaps one that has some psychological basis. The moment at which Elizabeth finds that she 'honestly' has started to love Darcy coincides with her almost certainly losing him as a result of the latest Bennet family disaster. Another irony – this might be comic, though again it seems wholly credible – is the discrepancy between what passes in the heart and mind of our heroine, and according to his appearance in Darcy too, and their politeness to each other. Neither of them is so overwhelmed as to forget the nicety of apologising for not fulfilling their social engagements. Reasonableness must regulate even disasters like this.

The elopement of Lydia is indeed a melodramatic event, though one that has been carefully prepared for. It is a 'wretched mistake' that Elizabeth did not publicise (or 'dishonour') the wickedness of Wickham. Jane and she discussed the matter, and decided against it, as the militia was just leaving Meryton. Had Elizabeth made public her knowledge of Wickham, her family might have been protected from this disaster. We will discover as the novel progresses that Darcy also blames himself for concealing Wickham's true character. Wickham's intrigue with Georgiana remains a shared secret between Elizabeth and Darcy throughout the whole second half of the book. On the one hand, Austen seems to be arguing for a greater honesty about sexual mores, or, at least, the perfidy of male scoundrels; on the other hand, the indiscretions of a young girl should be wholly sealed from public notice.

It may be difficult for a reader in the twenty-first century, with its very different ideas about sexual behaviour and morality, to take seriously the idea that 'Lydia's infamy' will cause her to be 'lost forever'. The way Austen writes about Lydia's running away suggests a double view about possible sexual relations before marriage. If the couple marry, their indiscretion may be ignored or eventually forgotten. If they do not marry, the woman's future is in jeopardy, while the man may probably carry on as he pleases. Marriage is the essential factor in the sexual habits described in *Pride and Prejudice*.

Primogeniture, the right of the eldest son to inherit property, title and power to the exclusion of all others – a social system likely to value the virginity of brides – is always in the background of *Pride and Prejudice*. Colonel Fitzwilliam is the typical younger brother: 'younger sons cannot marry where they like' (Chapter 33). Wickham passes himself off as a similarly disappointed male, cheated by the power of the favoured heir (though, of course, without any justification). The entail, a result of the view that only males should inherit property, hovers over the Bennet women. The possession of money and power, inherited wealth and property, or the lack of such privileges, are of the most acute significance in the society Austen depicts. It is bad enough that Lydia has thrown herself away on someone with neither wealth nor the diligence required for a career. Worse is Elizabeth's certainty, which is expressed soon after this passage, that Wickham has no intention of marrying her.

Towards the end of the passage there are two sentences of peculiarly heavy authorial commentary on the significance of Elizabeth's 'change of sentiment'. The narrator questions whether 'gratitude and esteem', the new 'foundations of affection' for Darcy, are sufficient and proper. The narrator shows a dual concern for psychological realism and morality ('neither *improbable* nor *faulty*') in thinking about Elizabeth's change. Then, in a curiously awkward construction, a conclusion is drawn about human behaviour. Regard springing from 'gratitude and esteem' might be 'unreasonable or unnatural' – another interesting pairing of words – but the sentence construction implies that it is not. Natural and reasonable regard is compared with another kind of affection: 'what so often described as arising on a first interview with its object, and even before two words can be exchanged'. In other words the 'love at first sight' (or at least, sexual attraction), that is the stock-in-trade of the sentimental romantic fiction that *Pride and Prejudice* seeks to correct. Though **ironically** described as the more 'interesting mode of attachment', love based on appearance, immediate sexual attraction, must be distrusted. Elizabeth's 'partiality' for Wickham, built on the immediate impression of his charming manner, on appearance, met with 'ill-success'. One wonders why Austen, who can be so linguistically deft, hedges and complicates this narratorial comment with 'if', 'but' and 'otherwise', and such awkward **circumlocutions**. Is this heavy humour, or a wish to discuss in a guarded way the key thematic interest in modes of love? Having made Elizabeth detest Darcy for half the novel, now she has to explain the way in which her better judgement has been formed by such unglamorous feelings as 'gratitude and esteem'.

# PART FIVE

# Background

## Biographical note

Jane Austen's father, George Austen, was rector of Steventon in Hampshire where Jane was born on 16 December 1775. She was the seventh of eight children, all boys except for her sister Cassandra who was two years older than her. The social status of the family was not unlike that of the Bennet circle in *Pride and Prejudice*, that is to say gentry, rather than aristocracy. The Austens and their neighbours the Digweeds were the two principal families of Steventon, but there were many other similar families in the neighbourhood.

Jane Austen only received scanty schooling. She and Cassandra were sent away when Jane was only seven, first to Oxford, finally to Reading. She returned home four years later, and spent the rest of her life living in her family. The schools she attended were not good. However, her father was a scholarly man and he tutored the sons of various wealthy neighbours for entry to Oxford and Cambridge. Books, including novels, were a common topic of conversation in the family. Jane's 'accomplishments' included singing and playing the piano, and needlework of the kind admired by Bingley. She could read French. The Austen family were keen amateur actors, and set up a theatre in the rectory barn. They were also busy correspondents: much of what we know about Jane Austen is derived from their letters, of which only about 160 survive from the thousands that they wrote.

In Steventon, Jane wrote a considerable amount of juvenile fiction, mostly **parodies**. *Love and Friendship* (finished 1790) is a mockery of the distorted passions and conventions of sentimental fiction. Between 1796 to 1797 she wrote *First Impressions*, the lost original of *Pride and Prejudice*.

When Jane was twenty-six her father retired and the family moved to Bath, which she did not like. Five years later after the death of her father she and her sister and their mother moved to Chawton, near Alton in Hampshire. Their house (now preserved as a small and interesting (!) museum), was near the estate of their brother Edward, who had been adopted by a childless aristocrat.

Both Cassandra and Jane received offers of marriage during their youth. In order to protect her sister's private life after her death, Cassandra censored the family letters, destroying many, and so the details of their relationships are vague. Scholars have tried to pin down various events. It seems likely that in 1802 Jane agreed to marry a wealthy man somewhat younger than herself called Harris Bigg-Wither, but changed her mind during the night, and refused him. Two or three other men seem to have featured in her life at various times, including a seaside romance with someone who died.

At Chawton, Jane resumed her literary interests. *Sense and Sensibility*, a reworked version of an earlier novel, was published anonymously in 1811. This was followed by *Pride and Prejudice* in 1813, *Mansfield Park* in 1814, and *Emma* in 1815, all published anonymously. She seems to have had no interest in declaring herself as an author, and avoided literary circles. Jane had suffered stoically for some time from a kidney illness, now thought to be Addison's disease. She died in 1817 in Winchester. Her last remaining novels, *Persuasion* and *Northanger Abbey* were published after her death with a 'Biographical Notice' by her brother Henry, this being the first occasion that the public learnt her name, and anything about her.

## Austen's other works

Austen's juvenilia were skits and **satires** for the amusement of her family. Her first published novel *Sense and Sensibility* was a re-working of an earlier **epistolary** draft called *Elinor and Marianne*. *Northanger Abbey* is a spirited parody of the Gothic novel. *Mansfield Park* is a strange and somewhat moralistic book, quite different in tone from the early works, an attempt to write about a weak and unattractive but morally good heroine, Fanny Price. In *Emma* Austen describes the matchmaking and misapprehensions of a wealthy, clever but slightly spoilt young woman, and her eventual getting of wisdom. *Persuasion* concerns the protracted courtship of a naval officer and the gentle, intelligent Anne Elliot, who is unloved by her snobbish father and sister. It is more gently concerned with the evaluation and description of feeling than the early novels. All these novels conclude with at least one marriage.

The first influences on Jane Austen's prose **style** would have been the Bible and the Book of Common Prayer. She read many books in her father's library, which was well stocked with classical authors. She seems to have particularly admired Dr Johnson (1709–84), and the novels of Samuel Richardson (1689–1761). In *Pamela* (1740) and *Clarissa* (1748) Richardson portrayed through their letters the anguish of distressed females. *Sir Charles Grandison* (1754) achieved a new depth and subtlety in characterisation. Such works provide models for Austen's interest in the minds and feelings of her characters.

She also read *Tom Jones* (1749) by Henry Fielding (1707–54): possibly Wickham's story of ill treatment by Darcy echoes the **plot** of *Tom Jones*, in which the hero Jones is ousted from the affections of Squire Allworthy by the nasty Blifil. In its balanced style, in the **satire** of its **caricatures**, and in its moral concerns, *Pride and Prejudice* has many affinities with eighteenth-century literature, which valued moderation, order, common sense and reason, and liked to laugh at the folly of those who did not aspire to these values.

Notwithstanding the range of eighteenth-century fiction, the novel was still perceived as a relatively new and suspect form in the early nineteenth century. People like Mr Collins did not regard it as serious literature, unlike for example sermons, essays or poetry. The development of lending libraries in the mid-eighteenth century (there is one in Meryton) made novels widely available, and new kinds of novel were written to cater for this taste. Aspiring women authors saw writing as a means of supporting themselves. Anne Radcliffe (1764–1823), for example, was paid £500 for the first publication of *The Mysteries of Udolpho* (1794), and £800 for *The Italian* (1797), both Gothic novels. Other women novelists of the time include Charlotte Smith (1749–1806), Fanny Burney (1752–1840) and Maria Edgeworth (1767–1849). Their novels centre on provincial and domestic life, providing another element in Austen's repertoire. Austen read widely amongst these and other writers of all kinds. The principal male novelist of Austen's time, Sir Walter Scott (1771–1832), had yet to publish: his first novel, *Waverley*, came out anonymously in 1814, a year after *Pride and Prejudice*.

Austen was also reading poets such as George Crabbe (1754–1832), Sir Walter Scott (1771–1832), Lord Byron (1788–1824) and Robert

Burns (1759–96). From this she would have learned the centrality of feeling in literature, and seen new ways of expressing it in language (this influence is observable in *Persuasion*). However in her early novels she is more apt to mock the new focus on 'sensibility'. The variety of her novels shows a determined interest in developing the form of the novel, and a desire to experiment with new techniques and subject matter.

# HISTORICAL BACKGROUND

The officers of the militia are conscripts: it is a non-professional regiment of soldiers. Though their arrival causes such a stir in Meryton, *Pride and Prejudice* gives little sense of a country at war with revolutionary France. 'The restoration of peace' mentioned in the final chapter refers to one of the short intervals in the European war, which had seen Britain cut off from Europe. From 1804 Martello towers (some still standing), were built along the south and east coasts as defence against possible invasion by Napoleon.

War with France had dampened revolutionary idealism in Britain. But British society was in the midst of various and far-reaching change: a centuries-old agricultural economy was being replaced by city-based industry. Especially in the north of England (which Austen never visited) factories, with machinery powered by steam, were taking over from domestic production. Fortunes were being made in textiles, iron and steel, mining, and pottery; and industry was creating a new urban working class. In religion Wesley's Methodists finally broke with the Church of England in 1795. At their huge open-air evangelical meetings they emphasised the urgency of individual salvation and the love of God.

*Pride and Prejudice* does not focus on these changes, but they do underlie some of the book's premises. Lady Catherine's and Darcy's snobbery is not a sign of their confidence, and might be seen as a last effort by the old land-owning class to protect their rights and interests. The sneering attitude of Caroline Bingley to 'trade' – though we are told this is how her father made money in the north of England – indicates a nervousness about class boundaries that is a symptom of the social changes underway. Darcy's friendship with Bingley is an alliance of old gentry with the new would-be gentry; intermarriage would seal the pact.

Mr Collins is a portrait of all the worst traits of the Church of England and its clergy. The 'livings' are in the whimsical control of land-owners like Darcy and Lady Catherine. Collins seems wholly insensitive to any spiritual aspect in his role. We hear nothing of his work in the parish. Like Elizabeth, the reader is shocked that Wickham could contemplate taking up his living in the Church. In what kind of religious institution can men like him easily find a career? In this context, the successes of Methodism are scarcely a matter of surprise.

# PART SIX

# C RITICAL HISTORY & BROADER PERSPECTIVES

## E ARLY CRITICAL RECEPTION

*Pride and Prejudice* is presumed to have sold quite well: selling for eighteen shillings (about 90 pence) for the three volumes, the first edition of 1813 was followed by a second edition in the same year, and a third in 1817 (it is not known how many were printed). However, critics in the journals did not take much notice of Austen's anonymous work. An exception is Sir Walter Scott's essay in praise of *Emma* in the *Quarterly Review*. Another early article in the *Quarterly Review* (1821) by Archbishop Richard Whately in attempting to justify the serious discussion of novels, notes that Austen's combine 'instruction with amusement'.

Charlotte Brontë thought her 'incomplete': 'the Passions are perfectly unknown to her'. In partial agreement with this kind of view, the influential critic George Henry Lewes wrote an article on 'The Novels of Jane Austen' in *Blackwood's Magazine* in 1859. He comments on her continued readership and survival after more popular novelists such as Maria Edgeworth had gone out of fashion. He admired in her 'the economy of art' without 'superfluous elements'.

The publication of *A Memoir of Jane Austen* by her nephew Edward Austen-Leigh in 1870 suddenly led to a burst of interest in both Jane Austen's life, which was previously unknown, and her novels. Unfortunately it led to the sentimentalisation of Austen, who was remodelled to fit the worst Victorian taste, as a decorous spinster genius. Out of this biographical approach grew the Janeites, fanatical admirers obsessed with every detail of the books and the author's life, and resistant to any sensible appreciation of her intelligence as a novelist. Henry James called their effusions 'pleasant twaddle', but because the Janeites polarised opinion the critical understanding of Austen became distorted. Many studies of her were written and some of a high quality, but the cult of Jane was overwhelmingly powerful.

Eventually the publication of a serious academic study, *Jane Austen and her Art* (1939) by Mary Lascelles put Austen criticism on a new professional footing. Lascelles countered Henry James's view that Austen was merely 'instinctive and charming' by analysing the artfulness of her composition.

In the university curriculum Austen quickly gained a remarkable ascendance. Two influential works placed her centrally in the **canon** of great novelists. F.R. Leavis's *The Great Tradition* (1947) famously argued that Austen was no less than 'the inaugurator of the great tradition of the English novel'. Ian Watt's *The Rise of the Novel* (1957) saw her as the final logic of the eighteenth-century novel.

In the last half of the twentieth century there was an enormous quantity of academic critical writing about Austen. It is impossible here to do justice to the variety of different kinds of study. Three approaches though have been chosen to indicate some of this variety. Early criticism of Austen is brought together in *Jane Austen: The Critical Heritage* (Routledge, London and New York, 1968).

# THE NEW CRITICISM

The critical movement called New Criticism originated in the 1930s and 1940s in the USA, but dominated the academic study of literature there and in Britain from the 1950s until the 1970s. F.R. Leavis took many of his assumptions from the New Critics. They based their methods on the study of lyric poetry. Anxious to escape from the narrow biographical or amateur historical approaches, they isolated the literary text from its surrounding context of history and politics, and contemplated its design and structure for its own sake. Close reading of individual, autonomous texts dominated teaching and scholarship. The observation of linguistic effects, such as ambiguity, **irony**, **paradox**, image and symbol, came to be the sole task of the reader. There are many such studies, and many of them present interesting and subtle views of the novels. Among the best is Barbara Hardy's *A Reading of Jane Austen* (Owen, London, 1975).

One particular study of Austen's *Mansfield Park*, an essay by the American liberal critic Lionel Trilling in *The Opposing Self* (Secher and Warburg, London, 1955), deserves special mention because it sets an agenda for the examination of all her novels, including *Pride and Prejudice*. His high claims for Austen show the internal, private nature of the reading process, and its application to the self.

The belief that values and ideas and behaviour are universal has now given way to a different set of premises. 'Value' itself is now regarded as the construction of particular cultures. There is no canon of great writing, no 'great tradition': texts are classified as 'great' for particular reasons at particular times. The so-called 'classics' of English literature were put on a pedestal to support the cultural *status quo*, forcing out texts that were subversive and radical, and that challenged the dominant political and social elitism.

From the 1980s till the present politics and history are now at the forefront of critical study. All language is deemed to be political, as it shapes the way in which we perceive the world. The study of Jane Austen's writing continues, and has still proved available to widely divergent views.

## Historicist criticism

Historicist critics adopt many different approaches, with the common aim of placing a text or a writer more clearly and exactly within their original context, political or cultural. A Marxist analysis of Jane Austen, for example, would seek to find evidence of Austen's attitude to the growth of the working classes, to class divisions, the role of servants, and the exercise of privilege.

One very influential and groundbreaking study placed Austen in relation to the political and ideological arguments of her time. This was Marilyn Butler's *Jane Austen and the War of Ideas* (Oxford, 1975, new introduction 1990). Austen's novels are examined for their engagement in the debates that raged between the Jacobins and the anti-Jacobins, the supporters and the opponents of French revolutionary ideas. According to this study, Austen was partisan and she was conservative. Her heroines willingly adopt traditional subservient female roles. In this Austen is contrasted with Maria Edgeworth, whose novels were more challengingly radical.

A more specialised and narrow study illustrating a historicist method is *Jane Austen and the Body* (Cambridge, 1992) by John Wiltshire. This examines eighteenth-century and present-day ideas of illness and in the light of these examines references in Austen's novels to illness, blushing, 'nerves' and sensibility. These prove to be remarkably frequent in her work, though there is no separate examination of *Pride and Prejudice*.

## FEMINIST CRITICISM

Feminist criticism examines the ways in which women (and men) are portrayed in novels, and considers the role of language and literature in relation to a culture and society which, most certainly in the time of Austen, and still nowadays, is dominated and created by men. It discovers groups of women writers, and female ways of writing, which have been ignored by the **canon**, and aims to re-assess the role of the woman writer in history.

Judgement has not stabilised with regard to Austen. Some feminist readers see her, like Butler (whose study predated the burgeoning of feminist writing), as the purveyor of feeble female acquiescence to the patriarchy. Others regard her as a subversive force for the good, mocking men and paying proper attention to the values of the female worlds that she describes.

Julia Prewitt Brown's *Jane Austen's Novels* (Cambridge, MA, 1979) explores her writing in relation to the cult of the family in the early nineteenth century, and shows how the values of womanhood and domesticity were dignified, strengthened and idealised by this.

Sandra M. Gilbert and Susan Gubar's *The Madwoman in the Attic: the Woman Writer and the Nineteenth-century Literary Imagination* (Yale University Press, New Haven, 1979) surveys women's writing in the light of their exclusion from the male dominated canon of literary greatness. Women writers have to find covert ways of subverting male culture, and Austen illustrates this in representations of female friendship, neurotic older women and weak fathers.

Two other works continue the examination of Austen's novels in relation to her contemporary culture. In *Jane Austen: Feminism and Fiction* (Harvest, Brighton, 1983) Margaret Kirkham examines the contemporary feminist controversies at the end of the eighteenth century. She finds that Austen implicitly espoused feminist views in her beliefs that women share the same moral nature and are as wholly responsible for their moral conduct as men. In *The Proper Lady and the Woman Writer*, by Mary Poovey (University of Chicago Press, Chicago,

1984), Austen's ideas of female propriety are compared to those of Mary Shelley and Mary Wollstonecraft.

## OTHER READING AND STUDY AIDS

A useful collection of essays and extracts is *New Casebooks: Sense and Sensibility and Pride and Prejudice*, edited by Robert Clark (Macmillan, Basingstoke, 1994). *The Jane Austen Handbook*, edited by J. David Grey (Athlone Press, London, 1986) contains a wide variety of diverse and interesting material. Jane Austen's letters are well worth reading: there is a new edition edited by Deidre Le Faye (Oxford University Press, Oxford, 1995).

| World events | Author's life | Literary events |
| --- | --- | --- |
| | | **1740** Samuel Richardson, *Pamela, or Virtue Rewarded* |
| | | **1748** Samuel Richardson, *Clarissa* |
| | | **1749** Henry Fielding, *The History of Tom Jones, a Foundling* |
| | | **1754** Samuel Richardson, *Sir Charles Grandison* |
| | | **1755** Samuel Johnson, *A Dictionary of the English Language* |
| | | **1757** John Home, *Douglas, A Tragedy* |
| | | **1758-60** Samuel Johnson writes *The Idler* series of essays |
| **1760** George III accedes to the throne | **1760** George Austen, Jane Austen's father, takes up trusteeship of a plantation in Antigua | |
| | | **1768** Laurence Sterne, *A Sentimental Journey Through France and Italy* |
| **1770** Captain James Cook discovers Botany Bay, Australia | | |
| | | **1771** Oliver Goldsmith, *A History of England;* Henry Mackenzie, *The Man of Feeling* |
| **1773** The 'Boston Tea Party': workers in Boston protest against British attempts to tax the American Colonies | | |
| **1775-6** American War of Independence breaks out, following the thirteen rebel colonies' declaration of independence from Britain | **1775** Birth of Jane Austen at Steventon, Hampshire | |
| **1777** France officially joins the Americans in the war against Britain | | |
| | | **1778** Fanny Burney, *Evelina* |

| World events | Author's life | Literary events |
|---|---|---|
| | | **1782** Fanny Burney, *Cecilia* |
| **1783** American independence is finally recognised by Britain | | **1783** Hugh Blair, *Lectures on Rhetoric and Belles-Lettres* |
| | | **1784** Death of Samuel Johnson |
| | | **1785** William Cowper, *The Task* |
| | | **1786** William Beckford, *Vathek: an Arabian Tale* |
| **1788** George III's first attack of madness | | **1788** First edition of *The Times* newspaper |
| **1789** Outbreak of the French Revolution; George Washington becomes first president of the United States of America | | |
| | | **1790** *Love and Friendship* finished |
| | **1791-2** The young Jane Austen writes *History of England* and *Lesley Castle* (both unpublished) | **1791** James Boswell, *The Life of Johnson* |
| **1792** France is declared a republic | | |
| **1793** France declares war on Britain during the ongoing French Revolutionary Wars; execution of Louis XVI and Marie Antoinette | | |
| | | **1794** Ann Radcliffe, *The Mysteries of Udolpho;* William Blake, *Songs of Innocence and Experience;* Prince Hoare, *My Grandmother* |
| **1795** Wesley's Methodists break with the Church of England | | |
| | | **1796** Matthew 'Monk' Lewis, *The Monk* |
| | **1797** *First Impressions* is rejected for publication; later rewritten as **Pride and Prejudice** | **1797** Anne Radcliffe, *The Italian* |

| World events | Author's life | Literary events |
|---|---|---|
| | **1797-8** An earlier work, *Elinor and Marianne*, is rewritten as *Sense and Sensibility* | |
| | **1798-9** Jane Austen writes *Lady Susan* (unpublished; later re-written and published as *Northanger Abbey*) | **1798** *Lovers' Vows*, an adaptation by Elizabeth Inchbald of August von Kotzebue's *Das Kind der Liebe*, first performed at Covent Garden |
| **1800-15** The Napoleonic Wars in Europe: a continuation of the French Revolutionary Wars led by Napoleon Bonaparte | | **1800** Death of William Cowper |
| **1801** The Act of Union creating the United Kingdom of Great Britain and Ireland comes into force | **1801** George Austen retires to Bath with his wife and two daughters; Jane and her sister Cassandra receive gifts of topaz crosses and gold chains from their sailor brother Charles | |
| | **1802** Jane Austen turns down Harris Bigg-Wither's proposal of marriage | **1802** The Pic Nic Society of dilettanti aristocratic amateur actors formed by Albinia, Countess of Buckinghamshire |
| | **1803** *Lady Susan* is bought by Crosby and Company but not published | |
| **1805** Nelson defeats a combined French and Spanish fleet at the battle of Trafalgar | **1805** Death of George Austen; Jane Austen abandons *The Watsons* | **1805** Walter Scott, *The Lay of the Last Minstrel* |
| **1807-8** Abolition Act outlaws Britain's slave trade | | **1807** George Crabbe, *The Parish Register* |
| **1808-14** Peninsular War in Spain between France and Britain | | **1808** Johann Wolfgang von Goethe, *Faust, Part I* |
| | **1809** Jane Austen settles at Chawton with her mother and Cassandra | **1809** First edition of the *Quarterly Review* published |
| **1811** King George III suffers his final attack of madness | **1811** *Sense and Sensibility* published; Jane Austen starts work on *Mansfield Park* | |

| World events | Author's life | Literary events |
|---|---|---|
| **1812** The Prince of Wales becomes Prince Regent; Prime Minister Spencer Perceval is assassinated in the House of Commons; Luddite riots spread throughout the Midlands and the North of England | | **1812** George Crabbe, *Tales in Verse* |
| | **1813** *Pride and Prejudice* published | |
| **1814** Allies invade France; Napoleon abdicates and retires to Elba | **1814** First publication of *Mansfield Park*; Jane Austen begins *Emma* | |
| **1815** Napoleon escapes from Elba to march on Paris, becoming Emperor again, only to be defeated by Wellington at the battle of Waterloo | **1815** Sir Walter Scott reviews *Emma* for the *Quarterly Review* | |
| **1815-23** John Nash builds Brighton Pavilion at the request of the Prince Regent | | |
| | **1816** *Emma* published; second edition of *Mansfield Park* appears; Henry, Jane Austen's brother, is declared bankrupt; Jane begins *Persuasion* in failing health | |
| | **1817** Death of Jane Austen at Winchester; *Sanditon* left unfinished; *Persuasion* and *Northanger Abbey* published posthumously | **1817** Walter Scott, *Rob Roy;* Lord Byron, *Manfred* |
| | | **1818** Mary Shelley, *Frankenstein* |
| | | **1819** Walter Scott, *Ivanhoe;* Lord Byron, *Don Juan* |
| **1820** Death of George III; the Prince Regent accedes as George IV | | |
| **1833** Slavery fully abolished in Britain | | |
| | **1870** Publication of nephew Edward Austen-Leigh's *Memoir of Jane Austen* | |

**abstract nouns** see concrete nouns

**antagonist** the opponent of the protagonist, the chief character in a play or novel, where two figures are engaged in a struggle with each other

**antithesis** a rhetorical term referring to the neat pairing of contrasting or opposite ideas in the same sentence

**aphorism** a generally accepted truth or principle expressed in a short and pithy sentence. Eighteenth-century poetry and prose is rich in aphoristic statements

**authorial intervention** a moment in a narrative when the narrator 'talks' directly to the reader rather than invisibly representing characters through their actions

**bathos** a laughable descent from the height of the elevated treatment of a serious subject, to the depths of ordinariness and dullness

**canon** originally a law of the Church; hence the list of books in the Bible accepted and genuine; and by further extension, those literary works which traditionally compose the 'great works' of a nation's literature. The assumption that some authors are intrinsically 'great' is now disputed, though canonical writers like Shakespeare and Jane Austen still feature in the National Curriculum

**caricature** a grotesque or ludicrous rendering of a character, in art or writing, achieved by the exaggeration of personality traits

**centre of consciousness** a term given by Henry James to the technique of telling a story wholly or chiefly from the point of view of one individual, though the narrative is still third-person, rather than first-person or autobiographical

**circumlocution** words and descriptions which take roundabout ways of approaching or hinting at a subject rather than addressing it directly, either for comic or ironic effect, or to avoid embarrassing topics

**concrete nouns** are words representing things and solid objects, such as 'hat', 'horse', or 'hazel-nut', as opposed to abstract nouns which stand for intangible ideas or feelings like 'happiness', 'history', 'hate', 'hope', etc

**dialogue** the speech and conversation of characters in any literary work

**dramatic irony** a common effect in drama (and by extension in novels too), referring to those moments when the audience (or reader) knows more about the circumstances and perhaps future of the characters that are being represented than those characters themselves do

**epistolary novel** a novel in which the story is told entirely through letters sent by those participating or observing the events

**figurative language** decorative language that departs from the plainest expression of meaning, by using 'figures of speech'. These are grammatical forms or ways of achieving expression or description that create those patterns or special effects which are common in literary writing. As metaphor is one of the commonest figures of speech, 'figurative language' sometimes refers to metaphorical language

**foreground** a term related to art, where some part of a picture is placed at the front of the imagined space perceived by the viewer. In literature a similar effect may be created by some special and noticeable feature of the language, such as a metaphor or similar figure of speech, or by its position in the literary work

**foreshadow** the capacity of a narrative to hint at or presage future events

**free indirect thought** or **speech** or **style** or **discourse** a way of representing a character's speech or thought that is neither direct speech with inverted commas, nor reported speech with the paraphernalia of 'he said that ...' etc.
  *Thought expressed as direct speech*: 'I must be collected and calm' she thought.
  *Thought expressed as reported speech*: She thought that she ought to be collected and calm.
  *Thought expressed in free indirect style*: She must be collected and calm.

**implied reader** every text contains features which hint at or imply the kind of reader at which it is aimed. These features may be to do with subject matter, tone of voice, assumptions as to shared interests and knowledge, etc

**irony** saying one thing while you mean another. A capacity for irony indicates a disposition to see things from several points of view (See also pp. 101–2)

**metaphor** a figure of speech in which an idea, action or thing is said actually *to be* something else, drawing out a resemblance between the two. Common in everyday speech – calling someone a 'rat' or a 'drone' or a 'flower' is metaphorical – and in literary writing, especially poetry

**motif** a topic raised at several points in a literary work, of lesser significance than a theme. Dancing, walking, reading, letter-writing, clothes and food all serve as motifs in Pride and Prejudice. Characters are distinguished from each other by their attitudes to such interests or activities

**omniscient narrator** the narrator of a story who knows in a godlike way every detail of the characters' lives, their motives, intentions, desires, thoughts, actions, etc

**paradox** an apparently self-contradictory statement, or one that seems in conflict with logic or opinion, yet expressing a meaning or truth behind the seeming absurdity

**parody** an imitation of a specific work of literature, or literary style or genre, devised so as to ridicule its characteristic features

**plot** the plan of a literary work, suggesting the pattern of relationships between events

**protagonist** the chief character in a play or novel, now almost synonymous with 'hero' or 'heroine', who may be locked in a struggle with the villain, or antagonist A word from Greek drama

**realism** a difficult and often vague term. Realism has come to refer to novels that attempt to describe characters in relation to their society, and therefore proceed with the premise that this attempt is possible and worthwhile. The characters and society are assumed to be 'normal' and examples of 'ordinary life', though such concepts are matters of dispute

**register** the kind of language being used

**satire** literature which exhibits or examines vice and folly and makes them appear ridiculous or contemptible

**style** the characteristic manner in which a writer expresses her- or himself, or the particular manner of an individual literary work

**subtext** the situation that lies behind the behaviour of the characters in a play or novel, but which is not referred to or explained explicitly

**theme** the abstract subject of a literary work: its central idea or ideas

Martin Gray is Head of the Department of Languages, Linguistics and Literary Studies at the University of Luton. He is the General Editor of the York Notes Advanced series, and author of *The Penguin Book of the Bicycle*, *A Dictionary of Literary Terms*, and *A Chronology of English Literature*.

Laura Gray is his daughter. She graduated in English Literature from Somerville College, Oxford, and currently works in Italy.

## York Notes Advanced (£3.99 each)

Margaret Atwood
*Cat's Eye*

Margaret Atwood
*The Handmaid's Tale*

Jane Austen
*Mansfield Park*

Jane Austen
*Persuasion*

Jane Austen
*Pride and Prejudice*

Alan Bennett
*Talking Heads*

William Blake
*Songs of Innocence and of Experience*

Charlotte Brontë
*Jane Eyre*

Emily Brontë
*Wuthering Heights*

Angela Carter
*Nights at the Circus*

Geoffrey Chaucer
*The Franklin's Prologue and Tale*

Geoffrey Chaucer
*The Miller's Prologue and Tale*

Geoffrey Chaucer
*Prologue To the Canterbury Tales*

Geoffrey Chaucer
*The Wife of Bath's Prologue and Tale*

Samuel Taylor Coleridge
*Selected Poems*

Joseph Conrad
*Heart of Darkness*

Daniel Defoe
*Moll Flanders*

Charles Dickens
*Great Expectations*

Charles Dickens
*Hard Times*

Emily Dickinson
*Selected Poems*

John Donne
*Selected Poems*

Carol Ann Duffy
*Selected Poems*

George Eliot
*Middlemarch*

George Eliot
*The Mill on the Floss*

T.S. Eliot
*Selected Poems*

F. Scott Fitzgerald
*The Great Gatsby*

E.M. Forster
*A Passage to India*

Brian Friel
*Translations*

Thomas Hardy
*The Mayor of Casterbridge*

Thomas Hardy
*The Return of the Native*

Thomas Hardy
*Selected Poems*

Thomas Hardy
*Tess of the d'Urbervilles*

Seamus Heaney
*Selected Poems from Opened Ground*

Nathaniel Hawthorne
*The Scarlet Letter*

Kazuo Ishiguro
*The Remains of the Day*

Ben Jonson
*The Alchemist*

James Joyce
*Dubliners*

John Keats
*Selected Poems*

Christopher Marlowe
*Doctor Faustus*

Arthur Miller
*Death of a Salesman*

John Milton
*Paradise Lost Books I & II*

Toni Morrison
*Beloved*

Sylvia Plath
*Selected Poems*

Alexander Pope
*Rape of the Lock and other poems*

William Shakespeare
*Antony and Cleopatra*

William Shakespeare
*As You Like It*

William Shakespeare
*Hamlet*

William Shakespeare
*King Lear*

William Shakespeare
*Measure for Measure*

William Shakespeare
*The Merchant of Venice*

William Shakespeare
*A Midsummer Night's Dream*

William Shakespeare
*Much Ado About Nothing*

William Shakespeare
*Othello*

William Shakespeare
*Richard II*

William Shakespeare
*Romeo and Juliet*

William Shakespeare
*The Taming of the Shrew*

William Shakespeare
*The Tempest*

William Shakespeare
*Twelfth Night*

William Shakespeare
*The Winter's Tale*

George Bernard Shaw
*Saint Joan*

Mary Shelley
*Frankenstein*

Jonathan Swift
*Gulliver's Travels and A Modest Proposal*

Alfred, Lord Tennyson
*Selected Poems*

Alice Walker
*The Color Purple*

Oscar Wilde
*The Importance of Being Earnest*

Tennessee Williams
*A Streetcar Named Desire*

John Webster
*The Duchess of Malfi*

Virginia Woolf
*To the Lighthouse*

W.B. Yeats
*Selected Poems*

## GCSE and equivalent levels (£3.50 each)

Maya Angelou
*I Know Why the Caged Bird Sings*

Jane Austen
*Pride and Prejudice*

Alan Ayckbourn
*Absent Friends*

Elizabeth Barrett Browning
*Selected Poems*

Robert Bolt
*A Man for All Seasons*

Harold Brighouse
*Hobson's Choice*

Charlotte Brontë
*Jane Eyre*

Emily Brontë
*Wuthering Heights*

Shelagh Delaney
*A Taste of Honey*

Charles Dickens
*David Copperfield*

Charles Dickens
*Great Expectations*

Charles Dickens
*Hard Times*

Charles Dickens
*Oliver Twist*

Roddy Doyle
*Paddy Clarke Ha Ha Ha*

George Eliot
*Silas Marner*

George Eliot
*The Mill on the Floss*

Anne Frank
*The Diary of Anne Frank*

William Golding
*Lord of the Flies*

Oliver Goldsmith
*She Stoops To Conquer*

Willis Hall
*The Long and the Short and the Tall*

Thomas Hardy
*Far from the Madding Crowd*

Thomas Hardy
*The Mayor of Casterbridge*

Thomas Hardy
*Tess of the d'Urbervilles*

Thomas Hardy
*The Withered Arm and other Wessex Tales*

L.P. Hartley
*The Go-Between*

Seamus Heaney
*Selected Poems*

Susan Hill
*I'm the King of the Castle*

Barry Hines
*A Kestrel for a Knave*

Louise Lawrence
*Children of the Dust*

Harper Lee
*To Kill a Mockingbird*

Laurie Lee
*Cider with Rosie*

Arthur Miller
*The Crucible*

Arthur Miller
*A View from the Bridge*

Robert O'Brien
*Z for Zachariah*

Frank O'Connor
*My Oedipus Complex and Other Stories*

George Orwell
*Animal Farm*

J.B. Priestley
*An Inspector Calls*

J.B. Priestley
*When We Are Married*

Willy Russell
*Educating Rita*

Willy Russell
*Our Day Out*

J.D. Salinger
*The Catcher in the Rye*

William Shakespeare
*Henry IV Part 1*

William Shakespeare
*Henry V*

William Shakespeare
*Julius Caesar*

William Shakespeare
*Macbeth*

William Shakespeare
*The Merchant of Venice*

William Shakespeare
*A Midsummer Night's Dream*

William Shakespeare
*Much Ado About Nothing*

William Shakespeare
*Romeo and Juliet*

William Shakespeare
*The Tempest*

William Shakespeare
*Twelfth Night*

George Bernard Shaw
*Pygmalion*

Mary Shelley
*Frankenstein*

R.C. Sherriff
*Journey's End*

Rukshana Smith
*Salt on the Snow*

John Steinbeck
*Of Mice and Men*

Robert Louis Stevenson
*Dr Jekyll and Mr Hyde*

Jonathan Swift
*Gulliver's Travels*

Robert Swindells
*Daz 4 Zoe*

Mildred D. Taylor
*Roll of Thunder, Hear My Cry*

Mark Twain
*Huckleberry Finn*

James Watson
*Talking in Whispers*

Edith Wharton
*Ethan Frome*

William Wordsworth
*Selected Poems*

*A Choice of Poets*

*Mystery Stories of the Nineteenth Century including The Signalman*

*Nineteenth Century Short Stories*

*Poetry of the First World War*

*Six Women Poets*

# FUTURE TITLES IN THE YORK NOTES SERIES

Jane Austen
*Emma*

Jane Austen
*Sense and Sensibility*

Samuel Beckett
*Waiting for Godot* and
*Endgame*

Louis de Bernières
*Captain Corelli's Mandolin*

Charlotte Brontë
*Villette*

Caryl Churchill
*Top Girls* and *Cloud Nine*

Charles Dickens
*Bleak House*

T.S. Eliot
*The Waste Land*

Thomas Hardy
*Jude the Obscure*

Homer
*The Iliad*

Homer
*The Odyssey*

Aldous Huxley
*Brave New World*

D.H. Lawrence
*Selected Poems*

Christopher Marlowe
*Edward II*

George Orwell
*Nineteen Eighty-four*

Jean Rhys
*Wide Sargasso Sea*

William Shakespeare
*Henry IV Pt I*

William Shakespeare
*Henry IV Part II*

William Shakespeare
*Macbeth*

William Shakespeare
*Richard III*

Tom Stoppard
*Arcadia* and *Rosencrantz and
Guildenstern are Dead*

Virgil
*The Aeneid*

Jeanette Winterson
*Oranges are Not the Only
Fruit*

Tennessee Williams
*Cat on a Hot Tin Roof*

*Metaphysical Poets*

# Notes

# Notes